Lonely planet

Pocket
DUBAI
TOP SIGHTS • LOCAL LIFE • MADE EASY

D1360212

Andrea Schulte-Peevers

In This Book

QuickStart Guide

Your keys to understanding the city – we help you decide what to do and how to do it

Need to Know
Tips for a smooth trip

Neighbourhoods
What's where

Explore Dubai

The best things to see and do, neighbourhood by neighbourhood

Top Sights
Make the most of your visit

Local Life
The insider's city

The Best of Dubai

The city's highlights in handy lists to help you plan

Best Walks
See the city on foot

Dubai's Best...
The best experiences

Survival Guide

Tips and tricks for a seamless, hassle-free city experience

Getting Around
Travel like a local

Essential Information
Including where to stay

Our selection of the city's best places to eat, drink and experience:

◉ **Sights**

✖ **Eating**

◗ **Drinking**

✪ **Entertainment**

🔒 **Shopping**

These symbols give you the vital information for each listing:

☏ Telephone Numbers	👪 Family-Friendly
⊙ Opening Hours	🚌 Bus
P Parking	⛴ Ferry
⊖ Nonsmoking	Ⓜ Metro
@ Internet Access	Ⓢ Subway
🛜 Wi-Fi Access	🚋 Tram
🥗 Vegetarian Selection	🚆 Train

Find each listing quickly on maps for each neighbourhood:

Bar Hemingway

16 ◗ Map p233, B2

Legend has it that Hemi
self, wielding a machine
...ate this timber-pan
...ered bar during
...showpiece is a
...en by Papa ar
... town. Dress
...s.com; Hôtel Rit
⊙ 6.30pm-2a

Lonely Planet's Dubai

Lonely Planet Pocket Guides are designed to get you straight to the heart of the city.

Inside you'll find all the must-see sights, plus tips to make your visit to each one really memorable. We've split the city into easy-to-navigate neighbourhoods and provided clear maps so you'll find your way around with ease. Our expert authors have searched out the best of the city: walks, food, nightlife and shopping, to name a few. Because you want to explore, our 'Local Life' pages will take you to some of the most exciting areas to experience the real Dubai.

And of course you'll find all the practical tips you need for a smooth trip: itineraries for short visits, how to get around, and how much to tip the guy who serves you a drink at the end of a long day's exploration.

It's your guarantee of a really great experience.

Our Promise

You can trust our travel information because Lonely Planet authors visit the places we write about, each and every edition. We never accept freebies for positive coverage, so you can rely on us to tell it like it is.

QuickStart Guide   7

Explore Dubai   21

Worth a Trip:

The Best of Dubai   **125**

Dubai's Best Walks

Dubai's Best ...

Survival Guide   **145**

QuickStart Guide

Welcome to Dubai

Dubai is gearing up to host World Expo 2020, but clued-in travellers know that this tiny powerhouse emirate has long been an exciting place to visit for foodies, fun seekers, shoppers, art lovers and desert rats. Whether it's the simple life or futuristic luxury, you'll be sure to find it in this peaceful outpost brimming with energy, optimism and openness.

Surfer on beach near Burj Al Arab (p70)
HOLGER LEUE / GETTY IMAGES ©

Dubai
Top Sights

Burj Khalifa (p86)

Shaped like a deep-space rocket, the world's tallest building also holds the records for the highest outdoor observation deck and the most floors.

Madinat Jumeirah (p68)

Marvel at the mythical old Arabian architecture of Madinat Jumeirah, with its mesmerising shops, entertainment venues and restaurants set around photogenic Venetian-style canals.

Gold Souq (p24)

For a shot of Arabian Nights flair, plunge into this charmingly chaotic warren of souqs shaded by a wooden lattice roof and teeming with dazzling jewellery and gems.

Burj Al Arab (p70)

This landmark luxe hotel, with its dramatic design that mimics the sail of a ship, floats on its own man-made island and has become the iconic symbol of Dubai's boom years.

Dubai Museum
(p40)

Housed in Al Fahidi Fort, the city's oldest surviving structure, this museum provides an excellent survey of Dubai's turbo evolution from desert settlement to 21st-century powerhouse.

Al Fahidi Historic District (p42)

Exploring this restored heritage area in Bur Dubai provides a tangible sense of historic Arabian architecture and culture. Some of the traditional buildings house museums, craft shops, galleries, guesthouses and cafes.

Dubai Mall (p84)

Hang on to those purse strings or give in to temptation at the world's largest mall, packed with such fun diversions as a giant aquarium, an indoor theme park and a huge dino skeleton.

Abu Dhabi (p122)

Dubai's neighbouring emirate makes for a lovely day trip. Feast your eyes on the country's most ornate mosque, keep tabs on the upcoming Cultural District and relax on the sandy beaches.

Dubai
Local Life

Insider tips to help you find the real city

After checking out Dubai's top sights, here's how you can experience what makes the city truly tick. Connect with your inner glutton at a Friday brunch, keep tabs on Middle Eastern art on a gallery hop, or take a leisurely saunter along the marina. All are features that make up the locals' Dubai.

Let's Do Brunch
(p120)

▶ Sociable gathering
▶ Diverse cuisine

Meeting friends for a gut-busting all-inclusive Friday brunch is a time-honoured tradition in Dubai. Restaurants, many of them in the five-star hotels, outdo each other with table-bending buffets of global delicacies, live cooking stations, cheese and dessert rooms, and enough booze to fuel a party in Vegas.

Gallery Hopping around Al Quoz
(p72)

▶ Artistic inspiration
▶ Urban landscapes

Tear yourself away from the beach or mall and find out why the art scene in Dubai is buzzing. Start by perusing the white cube warehouse galleries of Al Quoz, a gritty industrial area. It's a great way to familiarise yourself with an artistic vision still relatively unknown outside the Middle East.

The Marina Walk
(p104)

▶ Relaxed vibe
▶ Family fun

Nobody walks in LA, and the same could be said about Dubai. Except, that is, at the scenic Dubai Marina where you can promenade along the waterfront amid sleek yachts and a phalanx of high-rises, perhaps stopping for coffee or a bite in a charismatic restaurant or *sheesha* (water pipe) lounge.

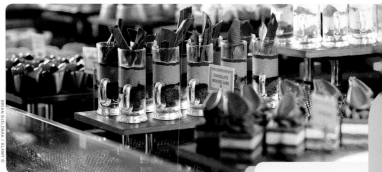

Selection of desserts on display at Al Qasr Hotel (p120)

Alserkal Avenue warehouse complex (p73) in Al Quoz

Other great experiences and insights to help you enjoy Dubai like a local:

Deira Fish Market (p32)

Bacchanalian Boating (p52)

Desert Safaris (p54)

'Liming' with the locals (p64)

Farmers Markets (p92)

Nostalgic Cruising (p110)

Dubai
Day Planner

Day One

One day in Dubai? Kick it off by following our **Bur Dubai Waterfront Walk** (p128) past some of the city's oldest buildings in the **Al Fahidi** (p42) and **Shindagha** (p46) historic districts, as well as a mosque, a souq and a Hindi temple. Hop on an *abra* (wooden ferry) across to Deira to peruse exotic potions in the **Spice Souq** (p28), dazzling jewellery in the **Gold Souq** (p24) and wriggling fish in the **Fish Market** (p32), then board the metro at Palm Deira.

Arriving in skyscraper-studded Downtown Dubai, you'll feel catapulted from the past to the future. Make a beeline to the massive **Dubai Mall** (p84), home to the **Dubai Aquarium** (p85), **Dubai Dino** (p85) and an Olympic-sized **ice rink** (p91). The mall is dwarfed by the sky-piercing **Burj Khalifa** (p86), which you should ideally ascend around sunset (book way ahead). Afterwards marvel at the dancing **Dubai Fountain** (p85).

Take a taxi to Madinat Jumeirah for a romantic dinner with Burj Al Arab views at **Pierchic** (p77), then finish up with quiet drinks at **Bahri Bar** (p79) or a more lively vibe at the **Left Bank** (p79).

Day Two

Get up in time to join the guided 10am tour of the gorgeous **Jumeirah Mosque** (p62), the only one in Dubai open to non-Muslims. Stay for the Q&A, then ponder your experience over coffee at the **Lime Tree Cafe** (p64). Embark on a boutique-hop down Jumeirah Rd as far as **Mercato Mall** (p65), then find out what traditional Emirati cuisine is all about during lunch at **Al Fanar** (p62).

Dedicate the afternoon to slothdom. Head to the Dubai Marina and stake out a spot on the beach, either for free at **JBR Open Beach** (p108) or by luxuriating at the sophisticated **Meydan Beach Club** (p110). Rinse off the salt and sunscreen lotion before showing off the day's glow during happy hour cocktails at **Bliss Lounge** (p117) or **Pure Sky Lounge** (p118).

For dinner, decide whether you're in the mood for a view of the Gulf or the bobbing yachts in the marina. Good choices include **Asia Asia** (p112) or **Aquara** (p112). A great spot to wind down the night in style is on the breezy terrace of **Siddharta** (p117) at the Grosvenor House.

Short on time?
We've arranged Dubai's must-sees into these day-by-day itineraries to make sure you see the very best of the city in the time you have available.

Day Three

Greet the day with strong java and a healthy breakfast at **Tom & Serg** (p72), an ultrahip industrial loft cafe, before perusing the latest in Middle Eastern art on a gallery hop around the **Alserkal Avenue** (p73) warehouse complex in the industrial district of Al Quoz. Get a taxi to take you to the **Mall of the Emirates** (p76) where a must-see is **Ski Dubai** (p76), one of the world's largest indoor ski paradises.

Spend the afternoon keeping cool here or tackling slides, rivers and pools at the **Wild Wadi Waterpark** (p76). Dry off and pop back to Madinat Jumeirah to pick up cool souvenirs at the charming **souq** (p69) and take an *abra* tour around the resort's sweeping canal network. With its hard-to-beat location at the end of a long pier, **360°** (p78) is the shoo-in for best sundowner spot with the sensuously curved **Burj Al Arab** (p70) as a backdrop.

For dinner, try something different by booking a table at the **Act** (p97). Here you'll dine on Latin fare in a wild and velvety Victorian-style theatre while being entertained by singers, dancers, contortionists, acrobats and other cabaret-style performers.

Day Four

Make for Bur Dubai and the **Dubai Museum** (p40) to get a better understanding of the city's stratospheric rise from Bedouin village to hyper-modern megalopolis, but time your stay so you can catch the 11am **Dubai Ferry** (p46) for Dubai Marina. Have your camera primed for views of the Dubai coast as the boat plows through the turquoise Gulf waters, passing such landmarks as the Burj Al Arab and the Palm Jumeirah.

Stroll along the **Marina Walk** (p104) and watch the world on parade at a cafe over lunch. Check out the stores at the **Dubai Marina Mall** (p105), then hop on the tram and then the monorail and head out to the Palm Jumeirah. Commune with underwater creatures at the **Lost Chambers** (p108) aquarium at Atlantis The Palm.

Take a cab to the **101 Lounge & Bar** (p115) at the One&Only The Palm for sunset nibbles and drinks as the Dubai Marina skyscrapers turn into a twinkling phalanx. For dinner, catch the free shuttle boat to the One&Only Royal Mirage to take your taste buds on a magic carpet ride at **Tagine** (p112), an exotic Moroccan parlour.

Need to Know

For more information,
see Survival Guide (p145)

Currency
United Arab Emirates (UAE) dirhams (Dh)

Languages
Arabic, English

Visas
Citizens of 45 developed nations get free
30-day visas on arrival in the UAE.

Money
ATMs are widely available. Credit cards
are accepted in most hotels, restaurants
and shops.

Mobile Phones
Mobile phones operate on GSM900/1800.
Local SIM cards are easy to find and start
at Dh20. Both 3G and 4G networks are
available.

Time
Dubai is four hours ahead of GMT/UTC. The
time does not change during the summer.

Plugs & Adaptors
Electrical current is 220V. British-style three-
pin wall sockets are standard but many can
also accommodate European two-pin plugs.
North American plugs require an adapter and
possibly a transformer.

Tipping
Round up taxi fares to the nearest note; tip
waiters 10% to 15%, porters Dh5 to Dh10 and
valets Dh5.

① Before You Go

Your Daily Budget

Budget: less than Dh600

► Budget hotel room Dh300–400

► Indie eateries, food courts, supermarkets

► Public transport, happy hours, public
beaches, free museums

Midrange: Dh600–1200

► Double room Dh400–700

► Two-course meal in midrange restaurant
from Dh80 without alcohol

Top end: over Dh1200

► Four-star hotel room from Dh800

► Three-course gourmet meal with wine from
Dh400

Useful Websites

Lonely Planet (www.lonelyplanet.com/dubai)
Destination information, hotel bookings,
traveller forum and more.

Dubai Tourism (www.dubaitourism.ae)
Official tourism site.

RTA (www.rta.ae) Public transport information and trip planning.

Advance Planning

Three months or more before Double-
check visa regulations. Order tickets for
high-profile sporting and entertainment
events.

One month before Book tables at top restaurants and tickets for the Burj Khalifa and
Burj Al Arab. Check concert-venue websites.

One week before Check average daytime
temperatures and pack accordingly.

2 Arriving in Dubai

Taxis and the Dubai metro are both convenient modes of transport to/from the airport. Buses are slower and complicated to negotiate. If you are staying at a four- or five-star hotel, check if it offers airport transfers.

✈ From Dubai International Airport

Destination	Best Transport
Deira, Bur Dubai, Satwa	Metro to various stations between 5.30am and midnight (2am Fri & Sat) or Bus C1 from terminal 1 and 3 in the interim.
Madinat Jumeirah	Dubai metro to Mall of the Emirates, then taxi.
Dubai Marina	Dubai metro to Damac, then taxi.
Downtown Dubai	Dubai metro to Burj Khalifa/ Dubai Mall, then taxi as needed.

✈ At the Airport

Dubai International Airport The arrivals hall has ATMs and currency-exchange outlets, plus car hire and a tourist information desk. There are several restaurants in the departure lounges as well as a large duty-free store (there's also one in Arrivals) and shops. The nearest hotel, Dubai International, has one location on the arrivals level in Terminal 1 and another on levels five and six in Terminal 3.

3 Getting Around

Most visitors get around town by taxi. Note that cabbies navigate not by addresses but by landmarks (such as malls, big hotels, beaches etc). Check a map beforehand and try to be as precise as possible. The Dubai metro is an inexpensive, speedy and comfortable mode of transport. Buses offer good coverage but are slow and have baffling timetables.

Before hopping aboard public transport, you must purchase a rechargeable Nol card from ticket offices and vending machines in metro stations and some bus stations. Check www.nol.ae for the full scoop.

M Metro

The high-tech Red and Green Lines link all major sights, attractions and neighbourhoods between 5.30am and midnight Saturday to Wednesday (until 2am Thursday and Friday).

🚕 Taxi

Convenient, metered, fairly inexpensive and fast (except during rush-hour), taxis can be flagged down or boarded at ranks at shopping malls and hotels.

⚓ Boat

Abras (traditional wooden ferries) cross the Dubai Creek. The Dubai Ferry and water buses are good for sightseeing.

🚋 Tram

The Dubai Tram was launched in December 2014 and trundles along Al Sufouh Rd between Dubai Media City and Dubai Marina.

🚌 Bus

Buses can be overcrowded and slow, although long-distance buses generally have direct routes and are adequately comfortable.

Dubai's
Neighbourhoods

Burj Al
Arab

 Madinat
Jumeirah

**Dubai Marina &
Palm Jumeirah
(p102)**
Tailor-made for
hedonists, this area
entices with family-
friendly beaches, luxury
hotels, a pedestrian-
friendly marina and
some hot-stepping
nightlife.

Worth a Trip
◉ **Top Sights**
Abu Dhabi

**Burj Al Arab &
Madinat Jumeirah
(p66)**
This modern Arabian
village has superb
beaches, restaurants
and souvenir shopping
backed by the iconic
Burj.

◉ **Top Sights**
Madinat Jumeirah
Burj Al Arab

Jumeirah & Around (p58)
Hugging a fabulous stretch of beach, this villa-studded residential area also has plenty in store for fashionistas and adventurous eaters.

Bur Dubai (p38)
Dubai's historic hub is a polycultural potpourri of restored buildings, budget eateries, shopping bargains and photogenic Creek views.

👁 **Top Sights**

Dubai Museum

Al Fahidi Historic District

Dubai
Museum

Gold
Souq

Al Fahidi
Historic
District

Burj
Khalifa

Dubai
Mall

Downtown Dubai (p82)
The Burj Khalifa presides over the city's futuristic centre with plenty to delight shoppers, families and art and architecture fans.

👁 **Top Sights**

Dubai Mall

Burj Khalifa

Deira (p22)
Charismatic, crowded and cacophonous, Deira's twisting roads are loaded with atmospheric souqs, heritage sites and fantastic eats.

👁 **Top Sights**

Gold Souq

Explore
Dubai

Worth a Trip

Boat on Dubai Marina (p102)
KONSTANTIN BELINSKY / GETTY IMAGES ©

Explore

Deira

Hugging the northern side of the Bur Dubai Creek, Deira is one of Dubai's oldest and most charismatic neighbourhoods, a world apart from the sky-piercing towers of modern Dubai. Its most distinctive asset is the cluster of souqs (spice, gold, perfume, fish, produce) – a tangle of narrow lanes erupting with sounds and smells that bursts into life in the late afternoon.

The Sights in a Day

☀ Deira is famous for its souqs, and among the most photogenic is the **Fish Market** (p32), which is at its bustling best early in the morning. For a nose-pleasing antidote head to the **Perfume Souq** (p28) next and give the pungent Arabic scents a sniff. If you not only want to smell good but look good too, shop for pretty baubles in the nearby **Gold Souq** (p24) before treating yourself to a superb Persian lunch at **Shabestan** (p30).

☀ Get a sense of how wealthy Emiratis lived a century ago at the **Heritage House** (p28). It once belonged to a pearl merchant who also founded the **Al Ahmadiya School** (p28) next door. Both buildings have been exquisitely restored and now harbour small museums. Afterwards, stock your pantry with exotic herbs and spices at the nearby **Spice Souq** (p28).

☽ An atmospheric way to wrap up the day is with a dinner cruise aboard the **Al Mansour Dhow** (p32), a primped-up historic cargo vessel that presents you with views of the city skyline from the Creek. In the mood for a nightcap? Report to **QDs** (p34) for alfresco cocktails and *sheesha* (water pipe).

Top Sights
Gold Souq (p24)

♥ Best of Dubai
Eating
Al Tawasol (p30)
Shabestan (p30)
Aroos Damascus (p31)

Drinking
QDs (p34)
Irish Village (p34)

Non-Souq Shopping
Deira City Centre (p35)

Getting There

Ⓜ **Metro** Deira is served by both the Red and Green Lines; they intersect at Union station. The Red Line travels to the airport.

⚓ **Boat** *Abras* (wooden ferries) link the souqs in Deira and in Bur Dubai. A water bus travels further down the Creek to Baniyas from the Dubai Old Souq station.

Top Sights
Gold Souq

'Dubai: City of Gold' screams the banner atop the rainbow-coloured LED display at the wooden entrance gate to Dubai's Gold Souq. Moments later, you'll feel as though you've just entered a latter-day Aladdin's cave. Lining a wooden-latticed central arcade and its spidery side lanes are hundreds of jewellery shops spilling over with gold, diamonds, pearls, silver and platinum. Simple rings to intricate golden Indian wedding necklaces, it's a dazzling display and a must-see even for nonbling-brigade members.

◉ Map p26, B1

Sikkat Al Khail St

🕙10am-1pm & 3-10pm

Ⓜ Palm Deira

Entrance to the Gold Souq

Don't Miss

The Real Deal?

No need to worry about fakes at the Gold Souq. The quality of the gold is government-regulated, so you can be fairly confident that the piece of jewellery you've got your eye on is genuine (unlike the Rolex watches and Prada bags touts are trying to tempt you with). The price is determined by weight based on the official daily international rate as well as by the workmanship and the intricacy of the item. Sharpening your bargaining skills should make merchants drop the initial asking price by 20% to 30%.

Record-Breaking Gold Ring

If you're not buying, stop by the Kanz jewellery store at the northern souq entrance to snap a selfie with the world's largest and heaviest gold ring, as certified by none other than Guinness World Records. Called the 'Najmat Taiba' (Star of Taiba), the 21-carat beauty weighs in at nearly 64kg and is worth a hefty US$3 million.

People-Watching

Simply watching the goings-on at the souq is another treat, especially in the evening. Settle down on a bench and take in the colourful street theatre of hard-working Afghani men dragging heavy carts of goods, African women in bright kaftans balancing their purchases on their head, and chattering local women out on a shopping spree.

☑ **Top Tips**

▸ The best time to visit is in the bustling evenings; avoid sleepy afternoons.

▸ Credit cards are almost always accepted, but you'll get a better price with cash.

▸ If you don't see anything you like, don't panic. Most shops will custom-make something to your own design.

▸ Don't rush! Remember, you don't have to make a decision on the spot. Compare carefully before you buy.

✗ **Take a Break**

The shwarma at **Ashwaq** (Map p26, B2; ☎04-226 1164; cnr Al Soor & Sikkat Al Khail Sts; mains Dh4-7; ⏱8.30am-11.30pm; Ⓜ Palm Deira) rocks the palate. Wash it down with a freshly squeezed fruit juice.

THE GULF

500 m
0.25 miles

Al Khaleej Rd

8

Al Bahara
Hospital

Bahara St

AL
MUTEENA

Al Muteena St

Al Rasheed Rd

13

23A

19B

22B

13B

Al Khaleej
Roundabout

Burj
Roundabout

Al Khaleej Rd

Al Rasheed Rd

5B

3B

Salah
Al Din

12A

12

Baniyas Rd

Palm
Deira

Al Khaleej Rd

Al Khaleej Rd

Naif Rd

Omar ibn al Khattab Rd

22A

Al Jazeira St

Corniche

Deira Fish
Market

Al Khaleej
Roundabout

Al Nakhal St

Al Rigga Rd

27

Al Sakhra Rd

12 Al Daghaya St

10

14A

Naif Rd

Deira St

Naif Rd

Al Musallah Rd

NAIF

Baniyas
Square

Al Maktoum Hospital Rd

Union

34A

40A

57

Perfume
Souq

Souq

5

4

107

Covered
Souq

Souq

6

Al Burj St

26

Rd 14

Union
Square

15

18

14

10

Gold
Souq

Al Ras

Baniyas Rd

Al Ahmadiya School

Al Ras St

Sikkat al Khail St

Delta St

Spice
Souq

2

3

Dhow
Wharfage

Deira Old
Souq Abra
Station

7

Deira Abra
Station

Al Sabkha
Abra & Water
Bus Station

Baniyas
Water Bus
Station

Al Seef
Water Bus
Station

18

17

16

AL
RAS

Al Ghubaiba

Heritage House

1

Al Souq St

Dubai
Abra &
Water Bus Station

Old Souq Abra &
Water Bus Station

Al Fahidi
Historic
District

Al Fahidi St

Al Hisn St

Al Fahidi

Al Musallah Rd

Sheikh Khalifa
bin Zayed Rd

UMM
HURAIR

Shindagha
Historic
District

Al Shindagha Tunnel

Al Khaleej Rd

Al Shindagha Rd

Bur Juman

Khalid bin al
Waleed Rd (Bank St)

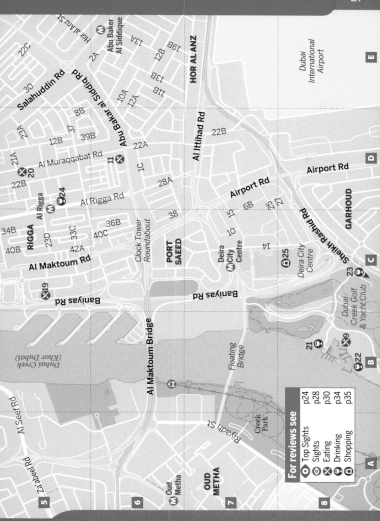

Dubai International Airport

Hor Al Anz St

Abu Baker Al Siddique

13A

22C

198

12B

2A

30

Salahuddin Rd

Abu Baker al Siddiqi Rd

23A

12B

37

8B

39B

13B

10A

12A

HOR AL ANZ

21A
20
22B

Al Muraqqabat Rd

11

Al Ittihad Rd

22A

22B

Airport Rd

1C

28A

Airport Rd

GARHOUD

24

Al Rigga Rd

38

15

6B

25
27

Sheikh Rashid Rd

Al Rigga

M

34A

23D

33C

40C

36B

40B

42A

RIGGA

Al Maktoum Rd

Clock Tower Roundabout

PORT SAEED

10

14

Deira City Centre

Deira City Centre

M

25

23

19

Baniyas Rd

Baniyas Rd

Dubai Creek Golf & Yacht Club

Al Maktoum Bridge

Floating Bridge

21

9

22

Dubai Creek (Khor Dubai)

Za'abeel Rd

Al Seef Rd

Riyadh St

Creek Park

OUD METHA

Oud Metha

M

For reviews see

◆	Top Sights	p24
⊙	Sights	p28
⊗	Eating	p30
⊕	Drinking	p34
⊞	Shopping	p35

Sights

Heritage House
MUSEUM

1 Map p26, B1

This 1890 courtyard house offers a rare opportunity to peek inside the one-time residence of a wealthy pearl merchant. Built from coral and gypsum, it wraps around a central courtyard flanked by verandahs to keep direct sunlight out. Most rooms have audiovisual displays and use dioramas to recreate traditional aspects of daily life. (✆04-226 0286; Al Ahmadiya St; admission free; ⏰8am-7.30pm Sat-Thu, 2.30-7.30pm Fri; Ⓜ Al Ras)

Al Ahmadiya School
MUSEUM

2 Map p26, B1

Dubai's first public primary school was founded by the pearl merchant Sheikh Ahmed bin Dalmouk and welcomed its first pupils (all boys) in 1912. Decades later, Dubai's current ruler, Sheikh Mohammed, was among those who squeezed behind the wooden desks to learn the Holy Quran, grammar, Arabic calligraphy, mathematics, literature and astronomy. The classroom is still there today but overall exhibits are pretty basic, explanations meagre and the audiovisual components often not working. (✆04-226 0286; Al Ahmadiya St; admission free; ⏰8am-7.30pm Sat-Thu, 2.30-7.30pm Fri; Ⓜ Al Ras)

Spice Souq
MARKET

3 Map p26, B2

Steps from the Deira Old Souq *abra* station, the sound of Arabic chatter bounces around the lanes of this small covered market as vendors work hard to unload aromatic frankincense, dried lemons, medicinal herbs and exotic seasonings all photogenically stored in burlap sacks alongside dried fruit, nuts, fragrances and knickknacks. (btwn Baniyas Rd, Al Ras Rd & Al Abra St; ⏰roughly 9am-10pm Sat-Thu, 4-10pm Fri; Ⓜ Al Ras)

Perfume Souq
MARKET

4 Map p26, B2

Several blocks of perfume shops stretching east of the Gold Souq hardly warrants the title 'souq', yet these bustling stores sell a staggering range of Arabian *attars* (perfumes), *oud* (fragrant wood) and incense burners. (Sikkat Al Khail & Al Soor Sts; Ⓜ Palm Deira)

Covered Souq
MARKET

5 Map p26, B2

Despite the name, this souq is not really covered at all; it's more a warren of small shops in narrow lanes criss-crossing a few square blocks. Even if you're not keen on cheap textiles, faux Gucci, *kandouras* (casual shirt-dresses worn by men and women), washing powder and cheap trainers, you're sure to be wowed by the high-energy street scene. (btwn Al Sabkha Rd, 107th St & Naif Rd; Ⓜ Palm Deira)

Vendor at Naif Souq

Naif Souq
MARKET

6 Map p26, C2

Although the historic Naif Souq burned down in 2008 and was replaced by this mall-style version, it's still an atmospheric place to shop for bargain-priced fabrics, henna products, hair extensions, costume jewellery and local dresses, including *abeyyas* (full length black robes worn by women) and colourful kaftan-style 'maxi' (ie full-length) dresses. (btwn Naif South, 9a & Deira Sts; ⏰8.30am-11.30pm; Ⓜ Baniyas Square)

Dhow Wharfage
HARBOUR

7 Map p26, B2

For a glimpse of Dubai's long trading history, stroll down the Creek for pho-

togenic close-ups of brightly coloured dhows, precariously loaded to the hilt with everything from air-conditioners to chewing gum to car tyres. This type of long flat wooden vessel used in the Indian Ocean and the Gulf has docked here since the 1830s when the local Maktoum rulers established a free-trade port, luring merchants away from Persia. (along Baniyas Rd; Ⓜ Al Ras)

Al Mamzar Beach Park
BEACH

8 Map p26, E2

This lushly landscaped beach park consists of a string of five lovely sandy sweeps and comes with plenty of infrastructure, including a swimming pool, playgrounds, water sports rentals, barbecues, grassy areas and air-conditioned cabanas (per day Dh160 to Dh210, on Beach 4).

There are also sun loungers and umbrellas for rent but food outlets are minimal so you might want to bring a picnic. Mondays and Wednesdays are for women and children only. It's about 6.5km from the nearest metro station. (☑04-296 6201; Al Mamzar Creek, Deira; per person/car Dh5/30, pool adult/child Dh10/5; ⏰9am-9pm Sun-Wed, to 10pm Thu-Sat; MAl Quiadah)

Eating

Traiteur   FRENCH $$$

 Map p26, B8

A meal at Traiteur is pure drama, both on the plate and in the striking 14m-high dining room and raised show kitchen, where a small army of chefs elevates classic French bistro fare into a fine-dining experience. The rotisserie duck and the seafood platter are both outstanding. The menu indicates which fish are sustainable options so you can order responsibly. Superb Friday brunch. (☑04-317 2222; www.dubai.park.hyatt.com; Park Hyatt Dubai; mains Dh130-270; ⏰dinner Sun-Fri; MDeira City Centre)

Shabestan   IRANIAN $$$

 Map p26, C4

Dubai's top Persian outpost also scores high on the romance metre with a panorama of glittering lights unfolding over the Creek. Take your time as you tuck into slow-cooked lamb, charcoal-grilled kebabs or chicken dressed in a walnut-pomegranate sauce.

Traditional ice cream with saffron and rose water makes a worthy coda to a superb meal. (☑04-222 7171; Radisson Blu Hotel, Baniyas Rd; mains Dh105-155; ⏰lunch & dinner; MUnion, Baniyas Sq)

Al Tawasol   YEMENI $

 Map p26, D6

At this gem, the best seats are on the carpeted floor of your private Bedouin-style tent with a thin sheet of plastic serving as a 'table cloth'. It's famous for its chicken mandi, a spice-rubbed and oven-roasted bird served over a bed of rice and eaten with your hands (staff will bring a spoon upon request). It's next to the Ramee Hotel. (☑04-295 9797; Abu Bakar Al Siddiq Rd; mains Dh23-45; ⏰11am-1am; MAl Rigga)

Aroos Damascus

SYRIAN $

12 Map p26, D4

A Dubai restaurant serving Syrian food to adoring crowds since 1980 must be doing something right. One of our favourite dishes is *arayees* – a pita pocket stuffed with spice-laced ground lamb and grilled to crunchy perfection.

Great tabbouleh, huge outdoor patio, cool flickering neon. Busy until the wee hours. (☎04-227 0202; cnr Al Muraqqabat & Al Jazeira Sts; sandwiches Dh4-20, mains Dh15-60; ⊙24hr; Ⓜ Salah Al Din)

Al Baghdadi Home

IRAQI $$

13 Map p26, E4

On Al Muteena, one of Dubai's best, if lesser-known, walking streets, Al Baghdadi is one of several restaurants specialising in the national Iraqi dish called *masgouf,* a local carp seasoned with salt, tamarind and turmeric and spit-roasted in a round fire pit. This takes about 30 to 45 minutes, giving you ample time to nibble on the mezze. (☎04-273 7064; Al Muteena St; mains Dh35-85; ⊙7am-1am; Ⓜ Salah Al Din)

China Club

CHINESE $$

14 Map p26, C3

Sensuous silks and embroidered tapestries provide a classy backdrop for the authentic Cantonese and Sichuan cuisine at this 'club'. Feast on such standouts as Sichuanese spicy wok-fried lamb or crispy Peking duck carved and rolled tableside. The deepfried ice cream is a delicious finish. Lunchtime brings great-value yum

---

Understand
Dubai Creek

What the Tiber is to Rome and the Thames is to London, the Creek is to Dubai: a defining stretch of water at the heart of the city and a key building block in its economic development. The base of the local fishing and pearling industries in the early 20th century, the Creek was dredged in 1961 to allow larger cargo vessels to dock. The first bridge, Al Maktoum Bridge, opened two years later.

Known as Al Khor in Arabic, the broad waterway used to end 15km inland at the Ras Al Khor Wildlife Sanctuary (home to a flock of flamingos and other birds) but was extended 2.2km to the new Business Bay district in 2007. Another 3km extension – dubbed Dubai Canal – kicked off in December 2013 and will eventually link the Creek with the Gulf.

Four bridges, a tunnel and both Dubai metro lines connect the two banks, but by far the most atmospheric way to get across is the Dh1 ride aboard a motorised *abra*, a traditional wooden boat that travels between the Deira and Bur Dubai souqs in a quick five minutes.

cha. (☏04-205 7333; www.radissonblu.
com; Radisson Blu Hotel, Baniyas Rd; yum cha
Dh99, mains Dh45-165; ☺lunch & dinner; 🛜;
Ⓜ️Union, Baniyas Sq)

Miyako JAPANESE $$$

15 Map p26, D1

The cool minimalist dining room of
this excellent Japanese eatery feels very
Tokyo, with sleek surfaces of stainless
steel, *shoji* screens and a traditional
tatami room. The sushi is super fresh
and expertly cut, from the dark-red
tuna to the marbled salmon. For an
entertaining experience (read: knife-
juggling chefs), grab a seat at a communal teppanyaki table. (☏04-279 0302;
www.dubai.regency.hyatt.com; Hyatt Regency
Dubai; set lunch Dh80-95, dinner Dh65-270;
☺lunch & dinner; 🛜; Ⓜ️Palm Deira)

Local Life
Deira Fish Market

Follow your nose to Dubai's largest
and busiest **fish market** (Map p26,
C1; off Al Khaleej Rd; ☺5am-1pm Sat-Thu,
4-10pm daily; Ⓜ️Palm Deira), near Al
Shindagha Tunnel, where wriggling
lobsters, shrimp the size of small
bananas, metre-long kingfish and
mountains of blue crabs have been
hawked since 1988. Come either
early in the morning or in the evening, and wear sneakers or other
waterproof shoes. If you can't cook
your purchase, take it over to **Grill
& Shark** in the adjacent building
where cooks will prepare your fish
for a few dirham.

Xiao Wei Yang CHINESE $

16 Map p26, B4

Near Twin Towers, Xiao Wei Yang
works like this: pick a bubbling
herb-based or spicy hotpot base that's
placed on a hot plate on your table.
Create a dipping sauce from a mix
of satay, garlic, chilli and
spices. Choose a few ingredients (fish
balls, crab, tofu, lotus root, beef slices)
to cook in the cauldron. Dip and
enjoy! Cash only. (☏04-221 5111; Baniyas
Rd; hotpots from Dh26, ingredients Dh2-15;
☺noon-2am; Ⓜ️Union)

Ashiana by Vineet INDIAN $$$

17 Map p26, B4

The brainchild of Vineet Bhatia,
India's first Michelin chef, Ashiana
is one of Dubai's top ambassadors
of modern Indian cuisine. Instead
of run-of-the-mill curries, your
taste buds will be treated to such
delicately spiced concoctions as *raan
lucknowi* (slow-cooked, 48-hour
marinated lamb) and *kukkad biryani*
(pastry-encrusted chicken tikka with
pomegranate-mint raita), all beauti-
fully presented. (☏04-207 1733; www.
ashianadubai.com; Sheraton Dubai Creek
Hotel & Towers, Baniyas Rd; mains Dh75-205;
☺dinner daily, lunch Sun-Thu; 🗡; Ⓜ️Union)

Al Mansour Dhow INTERNATIONAL $$$

18 🍴 Map p26, B3

For a traditional (albeit touristy)
experience, book a table on this old
wooden dhow cheerfully decorated

Stalls at Deira Fish Market

with bands of twinkling lights and operated by the Radisson Blu Hotel. A house band plays on as you graze on the lavish buffet spread that's heavy on Middle Eastern and Indian choices before reclining with a *sheesha* in the upper-deck lounge. Board outside the hotel. (☎04-222 7171; www.radissonblu.com/hotel-dubaideiracreek; Baniyas Rd; 2hr dinner cruise Dh195; ⏰8pm; Ⓜ Union, Baniyas Sq)

Glasshouse Brasserie
INTERNATIONAL $$

19 Map p26, C5

As the name suggests, Glasshouse has vast picture windows overlooking palms and the Creek beyond. The kitchen does not attempt pyrotechnics here, relying instead on pimping up such comfort-food faves as onion soup, Caesar salad, chicken tikka masala, prawn linguine and fish and chips. (☎04-227 1111; Hilton Dubai Creek, Baniyas Rd; mains Dh75-135; ⏰7am-midnight; 🛜; Ⓜ Al Rigga, Union)

Qwaider Al Nabulsi
ARABIAN $

20 Map p26, D5

Behind the Vegas-style neon facade, this place looks at first like a sweets shop but actually has a full menu of Arabian delicacies. A top menu pick is the felafel *mahshi* whose crunchy and sesame-seed-coated skin seals in a fluffy filling coloured green from the addition of parsley and other herbs. It's near Al Jazeira St. (☎04-227 7760; Al Muraqqabat St; snacks Dh10-17, mains Dh28-50; ☺7.30am-1am; Ⓜ Al Rigga, Salah Al Din)

Drinking

QDs

BAR, SHEESHA

21 🍺 Map p26, B8

Watch the ballet of lighted dhows floating by while sipping cocktails at this always-fun outdoor Creekside lounge deck where carpets and cushions set an inviting mood. In summer, keep cool in an air-conditioned tent. Great for *sheesha,* but skip the food (except for the pizza and Friday afternoon barbecue). (☎04-295 6000; www.dubaigolf.com; Dubai Creek Golf & Yacht Club, Garhoud; ☺5pm-2am Sun-Wed, to 3am Thu & Sat, 1pm-3am Fri; Ⓜ Deira City Centre)

Cielo Sky Lounge

BAR

22 🍺 Map p26, B8

Looking very much like a futuristic James Bond–worthy yacht, Cielo flaunts a sultry, romantic vibe helped by the bobbing yachts below and the cool Creek views of the Dubai skyline. It's great spot to ring in the night with tapas (great ceviche!) and sundowners (the sangria is a signature drink). Tuesday is ladies' night. (☎04-416 1800; www.cielodubai.com; Dubai Creek Golf & Yacht Club; ☺4pm-2am; Ⓜ Deira City Centre)

Irish Village

PUB, BEER GARDEN

23 🍺 Map p26, C8

This always-buzzy pub, with its Irish-main-street facade made with materials imported straight from the Emerald Isle, has been a Dubai insti-

---

Understand
Buying Alcohol

One of the most common questions among first-time visitors is: 'Can I buy alcohol?' The answer is yes – in some places. When arriving by air, you can, as a non-Muslim visitor over 18, buy 4L of spirits, wine or beer in the airport duty-free shop. You can also drink alcohol in the bars and clubs that are generally attached to four- and five-star hotels. Expats can acquire an alcohol licence, which entitles them to a fixed monthly limit of alcohol sold in such places as the African & Eastern liquor stores and some branches of Spinney's supermarket. Note that visitors are not permitted to legally purchase alcohol in these places and staff is supposed to ask to see the licence.

The only store where visitors can officially buy alcohol without a licence is at the Barracuda Beach Resort in the emirate of Umm al-Quwain, about an hour's drive north of Dubai. Note that you are not officially allowed to transport alcohol through Sharjah, although most people just seem to take the risk anyway.

tution since 1996. There's Guinness and Kilkenny on tap, lawns around a petite lake, the occasional live concert and plenty of cheap, cheerful pub grub to keep your tummy happy (and brain balanced). It's located next to Dubai Tennis Stadium. (✆04-282 4750; www.theirishvillage.com; 31st St, Garhoud; ⏰11-1am Sat-Wed, to 2am Thu & Fri; 🛜; ⓂGGICO)

Juice World
JUICE BAR

24 🍺 Map p26, D5

Need some A.S.S., Man Kiwi or Viagra? Then head down to this upbeat Saudi juice bar famous not only for its 150 fantastically creative liquid potions but also for its outrageous fruit sculptures. There's an entire room of them: must be seen to be believed. The big outdoor terrace offers primo people-watching. It's next to Al Rigga metro station. (✆04-299 9465; www.juiceworld.ae; Al Rigga St; ⏰1pm-2am; ⓈAl Rigga)

Terrace
BAR

With its sleek design, floor-to-ceiling windows and canopy-covered deck, the Terrace (see **9** ✖ Map p26, B8) provides plenty of eye candy before you've even taken in the chic crowd or the dreamy sunset views across the Creek. A raw seafood bar provides a major protein kick, while the big selection of top-shelf vodka should help loosen any inhibitions. It's next to the Dubai Creek Golf & Yacht Club. (✆04-317 2222; www.dubai.park.hyatt.com; Park Hyatt Dubai; ⏰noon-1.30am; ⓂDeira City Centre)

Issimo
SPORTS BAR

Illuminated blue flooring, black-leather sofas and sleek chrome finishing lend an edgy look to this sports-and-martini bar (see **19** ✖ Map p26, C5). If you're not into sports – or TV – you may find the giant screens distracting. Good for an aperitivo before dinner at the hotel's highly regarded **Table 9** (✆04-212 7551; www.table9dubai.com; Hilton Dubai Creek, Baniyas Rd; 3-/4-/6-course dinner Dh300/350/425; ⏰6.30-11pm; 🛜🍴; ⓂAl Rigga, Union) or Glasshouse Brasserie (p33) restaurants. (✆04-227 1111; Hilton Dubai Creek, Baniyas Rd; ⏰3pm-1am; 🛜; ⓂAl Rigga, Union)

Shopping

Deira City Centre
SHOPPING MALL

25 🔒 Map p26, C8

Though other malls are bigger and flashier, Deira City Centre remains a stalwart for its logical layout and wide selection of shops, from big-name chains such as H&M and Zara to locally owned stores carrying quality carpets, souvenirs and handicrafts. (✆04-295 1010; www.deiracitycentre.com; Baniyas Rd; ⏰10am-10pm Sun-Wed, to midnight Thu-Sat; ⓂDeira City Centre)

Mikyajy
COSMETICS

You feel like you're walking into a chocolate gift-box at tiny Mikyajy (see **25** 🔒 Map p26, C8), the Gulf's home-grown make-up brand. Although developed for Middle Eastern skin tones, the vivid colours brighten up any face. (☎04-295 7844; www.mikyajy.com; 2nd fl, Deira City Centre, Baniyas Rd; ☺10am-10pm Sat-Wed, to midnight Thu & Fri; Ⓜ Deira City Centre)

Virgin Megastore

MUSIC

The enthusiastic sales staff at Virgin Megastore (see 25 Ⓐ Map p26, C8) are great at suggesting Middle Eastern music to take back home, from traditional *oud* music to Oriental chill-out. The selection is huge. Also check out the Arabian and Iranian DVDs. (☎04-295 8599; 2nd floor, Deira City Centre, Baniyas Rd; ☺10am-10pm Sat-Wed, to midnight Thu & Fri; Ⓜ Deira City Centre)

Ajmal

PERFUME

The place for locally made traditional Arabian perfumes and scented oils, family-owned Ajmal (see 25 Ⓐ Map p26, C8) was founded in India in the early 1950s. Its stores are always crowded with local women keen on finding their favourite among the 200 heady and complex fragrances filled into equally fancy jewel-encrusted bottles. Check the website for additional branches. (☎04-295 3580; www.ajmal perfume.com; Deira City Centre, Baniyas Rd; ☺10am-10pm Sat-Wed, to midnight Thu & Fri; Ⓜ Deira City Centre)

Al Washia

ACCESSORIES

Has all that bling got to you yet? If not, then you can glitter along with the best of them by picking up some accessories here (see 25 Ⓐ Map p26, C8), including twinkling tiaras, jewelled hairpins, dingle-dangle earrings, fancy clutch bags and a few surprises, such as cushion-cover embroidery sets with Middle Eastern themes. (☎04-295 0221; www. alwashia.com; Deira City Centre, Baniyas Rd; ☺10am-10pm Sat-Wed, to midnight Thu & Fri; Ⓜ Deira City Centre)

Gift Village

DEPARTMENT STORE

26 Ⓐ Map p26, B3

If you've spent all your money on Jimmy Choo shoes and at the Gold Souq

---

Understand
Pashmina: Telling Real from Fake

Women around the world adore pashmina shawls, which come in all sorts of wonderful colours and patterns. Originally made from feather-light cashmere, there are now many cheaper machine-made synthetic versions around. Before forking over hundreds of dirham, make sure you're buying the real thing. Here's the trick. Hold the fabric at its corner. Loop your index finger around it and squeeze hard. Now pull the fabric through. If it's polyester, it won't budge. If it's cashmere, it'll pull through – though the friction may give you a mild case of rope burn. Try it at home with a thin piece of polyester before you hit the shops; then try it with cashmere. You'll never be fooled again.

LINDA STEWARD / GETTY IMAGES ©

A pashmina stall

and need a new inflight bag, this cut-price place has a great range. It also stocks cosmetics, shoes, clothing, toys, sports goods, jewellery and superbly kitsch souvenirs, all imported from China, Thailand and Turkey and sold at wallet-friendly prices. (☑04-294 6858; www.gift-village.com; Baniyas Sq; ☉9am-1am Sun-Thu, 9am-noon & 2pm-2am Fri; Ⓜ Baniyas Sq)

Women's Secret   LINGERIE

This sassy Spanish label (see 25 ❸ Map p26 ,C8) is popular for its global-pop-art-inspired underwear, swimwear and nightwear. Expect anything from cute Mexican cross-stitched bra-and-pants sets to Moroccan-style kaftanlike nightdresses. (☑04-295 9665; 1st fl, Deira

City Centre, Baniyas Rd; ☉10am-10pm Sun-Wed, to midnight Thu-Sat; Ⓜ Deira City Centre)

Al Ghurair City   SHOPPING MALL

27 ❸ Map p26, C4

If seeing all those flowing robes has made you want your own *gutra* (white headcloth worn by men in the Gulf States), grab yours at this ageing mall. The place to shop for national dress, it offers stylish *abeyyas* and *shaylas* (black headscarves), quality leather sandals, and *dishdashas* (men's shirt-dresses) in shades of ivory, brown and grey. (☑04-295 5309; www.alghuraircentre. com; cnr Al Rigga & Omar ibn Al Khattab Rds; ☉10am-10pm Sat-Thu, 2-10pm Fri; Ⓜ Union, Salah Al Din)

Explore

Bur Dubai

Creek-hugging Bur Dubai provides an eye-opening journey into the city's past, both in the Dubai Museum and on a wander around the restored historical quarters of Al Fahidi and Shindagha. The streets of the surrounding Meena Bazaar district teem with authentic local eateries feeding expats from Nepal, India and Pakistan, creating a nirvana for adventurous foodies.

The Sights in a Day

☀ Start with a cultural breakfast at the **Sheikh Mohammed Centre for Cultural Understanding** (p48) for a rare chance to meet locals and eat home-cooked Emirati food. Delve further into local culture and history with a spin around the **Al Fahidi Historic District** (p42), dipping in and out of the various small museums and shops before finishing up with lunch at the enchanting **Arabian Tea House** (p50).

☀ Thus restored, head to the nearby **Dubai Museum** (p40) for an hour of peering into Dubai's past. Enjoy the short stroll to the breezy **Bur Dubai Souq** (p46) via the atmospheric **Hindi Lane** (p46), then continue north along the Creek to the **Shindagha Historic District** (p46) to check out the handsomely restored buildings and wrap up with a juice at **Kan Zaman** (p50).

☾ Cab it down to Wafi City for superb modern Middle Eastern fare at impossibly romantic **Qbara** (p49) followed by drinks in the lounge or partying at nearby **People by Crystal** (p53).

 Top Sights

Dubai Museum (p40)

Al Fahidi Historic District (p42)

♥ **Best of Dubai**

Eating
Qbara (p49)
Jaffer Bhai's (p49)
Kan Zaman (p50)
Special Ostadi (p50)

Drinking
George & Dragon (p53)
Kan Zaman (p50)

Dance Clubs
People by Crystal (p53)
Music Room (p54)

Shopping
Ajmal (p57)
Bateel (p55)

Getting There

Ⓜ **Metro** The Red and Green Lines intersect at BurJuman, with the latter continuing into historic Bur Dubai before crossing the Creek.

⚓ **Boat** *Abras* (wooden ferries) link Bur Dubai to Deira from two stations near the Bur Dubai Souq.

Top Sights
Dubai Museum

Unless some mad scientist invents a time machine, this museum is your ticket to learning about Dubai's stratospheric rise from Bedouin village to megalopolis and global centre of trade and tourism. It's housed in Al Fahidi Fort, built in 1799 and the oldest surviving structure in town. The crenelated citadel served as the residence of the local rulers until 1896 and went through stints as a prison and a garrison before becoming a museum in 1971.

◉ Map p44, E2

☎ 04-353 1862

Al Fahidi St

adult/child Dh3/1

🕓 8.30am-8.30pm Sat-Thu, 2.30-8.30pm Fri

Ⓜ Al Fahidi

Dubai Museum, housed in Al Fahidi Fort

Don't Miss

Multimedia Presentation

This is a real highlight, so make sure you grab a pew and watch. The 10-minute film includes some fascinating archival footage that vividly depicts just how far Dubai has come from the 1960s to today. The movie covers each decade with a pictorial tour of achievements, progress and historical milestones. It's entertaining, informative and just the right length.

Souq Dioramas

After the film, you'll cross the deck of a dhow and enter a mock souq with endearing dioramas depicting shopkeepers and craftspeople at work. Some are enhanced with light effects, historical photos and film footage. Other scenes illustrate traditional life at home, at the mosque, in the desert and at sea.

Pearl Diving Exhibit

Take a pic of a magnificent wooden dhow before spending some time in the fascinating pearl-diving exhibition and marvelling at the fact that divers wore merely a nose clip while descending to extraordinary depths. What really brings this part of the museum to life is the historical footage of the pearl divers at work.

Archaeological Finds

The highlight for many will be archaeology section, which showcases finds from ancient settlements at Jumeirah, Al Qusais and other local archaeological sites, believed to date back to between 2000 and 1000 BC. Don't miss the well-lit gallery opposite the gift shop, with displays of unearthed artefacts from the numerous tombs in the area. Highlights include a 5000-year-old bronze dagger and 2000-year-old jewellery.

CHRISTIAN KOBER / GETTY IMAGES ©

☑ Top Tips

▶ Visit early in the morning or late in the afternoon to avoid tour groups.

▶ Check out the courtyard walls, made with traditional coral and gypsum.

▶ Don't bother with a tour guide: exhibits are well explained in English.

▶ Take the kids! They'll love the sound effects, films and detailed dioramas.

▶ Skip the gift shop and head for the nearby souq instead.

✕ Take a Break

For a tasty breakfast or light meal, head to the courtyard of the charismatic **Arabian Tea House** (p50).

The best butter chicken is served at **Sind Punjab** (p52), the oldest family eatery in the Meena Bazaar.

Top Sights
Al Fahidi Historic District

Traffic fades to a quiet hum in the labyrinthine lanes of this nicely restored heritage area, formerly known as the Bastakia Quarter. Its narrow walking lanes are flanked by sand-coloured houses topped with wind towers, which provide natural air-conditioning. Today, there are about 50 buildings containing crafts shops, cultural exhibits, courtyard cafes, art galleries and two boutique hotels.

◉ Map p44, E2

btwn Al Fahidi St & Dubai Creek

admission free

M Al Fahidi

Al Fahidi Historic District

Don't Miss

Majlis Gallery

In an old wind-tower house, **Majlis** (☎04-353 6233; www.themajlisgallery.com; Al Fahidi St; admission free; ⏱10am-6pm Sat-Thu; ⓂAl Fahidi) was founded in 1989, making it Dubai's oldest fine-art gallery. It presents mainly paintings and sculpture created by international artists inspired by the region as well as high-quality pottery, glass and other crafts.

Coffee Museum

This small private **museum** (☎04-380 6777; www.coffeemuseum.ae; off Al Fahidi St; admission free; ⏱10.30am-6pm Sat-Thu; ⓂAl Fahidi) in a historic Emirati home offers an aromatic bean-based journey around the world and back in time. Learn about the origins of coffee, examine centuries-old grinders, pots, roasters and other implements and sample traditional Ethiopian or Turkish coffee prepared by staff in traditional costume. Upstairs are a reading room, a children's corner and a modern cafe.

Al Serkal Cultural Foundation

A rambling courtyard building provides a fitting setting for this **gallery** (☎04-353 5922; Heritage House No 79, off Al Fahidi St; admission free; ⏱9.30am-8pm Sat-Thu; ⓂAl Fahidi) displaying traditional and cutting-edge works by local and international artists. In the workshop in front, you can often see a master engraver at work.

Coin Museum

Near the district's imposing mosque, this small **museum** (off Al Fahidi St; admission free; ⏱8am-2pm Sun-Thu; ⓂAl Fahidi) presents a collection of around 500 rare coins from throughout the Middle East and North Africa.

☑ Top Tips

▶ Don't be shy about pushing open some of those heavy doors and finding out what's behind them.

▶ Shutterbugs should visit early in the morning or late in the afternoon for the best light conditions.

▶ Look for a short section of the old city wall from 1800, which looks a bit like a dinosaur tail.

▶ Admission to all museums and exhibits is free.

✗ Take a Break

Have a mint lemonade or meat-free meal in the charming courtyard **cafe** (p52) of the XVA heritage hotel.

Adventurous foodies should head to **Local House** (Map p44, E2; ☎04-354 0705; www.localhousedubai.com; Al Fahidi St; mains Dh25-55; ⏱11am-10pm; ⓂAl Fahidi), which made headlines in 2010 when it became the first Dubai restaurant to serve camel burgers.

Shindagha Historic District
Camel Museum
Heritage Village
Diving Village
Traditional Architecture Museum
Sheikh Saeed Al Maktoum House
Al Ghubaiba
Baniyas Rd
Al Ras
AL RAS
SHINDAGHA
Al Ghubaiba Rd
Falcon Roundabout
Al Falah Rd
Bur Dubai Souq
Dubai Old Souq Abra & Water Bus Station
Deira Old Souq Abra Station
Hindi Lane
Ali bin Abi Talib St
Al Fahidi St
Al Hisn St
Dubai Museum
Al Fahidi Historic District
XVA Gallery
Al Musallah Rd
Al Nahda St
Al Raffa St
Khalid bin al Waleed Rd
Khalid bin al Waleed Rd (Bank St)
Al Fahidi
Al Rolla Rd
BUR DUBAI
Kuwait St
Al Mankhool Rd
MANKHOOL
Wonder Bus Tours
Sheikh Khalifa bin Zayed Rd
Sheikh Khalifa bin Zayed Rd (Trade Centre Rd)
Burjuman
UMM HURAIR
Al Seef Water Bus Station
Al Mina Rd
AL JAFILIYA
Al Jafiliya
ADCB
Sheikh Rashid Rd
Jumeirah Rd
Department of Health & Medical Services

Sights

Bur Dubai Souq   SOUQ

 1 Map p44, D2

This covered souq may not be as old as the Deira souqs but it can be just as atmospheric – although be prepared for pushy vendors. Friday evenings here are especially lively, as it turns into a virtual crawling carnival with expat workers loading up on socks, pashminas, T-shirts and knock-off Calvins on their day off. In a section known as **Textile Souq** you can stock up on fabrics – silk, cotton, satin, velvet – at very reasonable prices.
(btwn Bur Dubai waterfront & Ali bin Abi Talib St; M Al Ghubaiba)

✅ Top Tip

Mini-Cruises

A great way to see the sights is on a **Dubai Ferry** (Map p44, D1; ☎ 800 9090; www.rta.ae; Al Ghubaiba Water Station, Shindagha Waterfront; gold/silver tickets Dh75/50, child 2-10yr half-price; M Al Ghubaiba) mini-cruise. Boats leave several times daily from the Creek near the Al Ghubaiba metro station. Options include a 90-minute one-way trip to Dubai Marina past Jumeirah, the Burj Al Arab and the Palm Jumeirah (11am, 1pm and 6.30pm); a one-hour afternoon-tea Creek cruise (3pm) and a one-hour sunset cruise to Jumeirah Beach (5pm). Soft drinks and snacks are available.

XVA Gallery   GALLERY

2 Map p44, E2

Tucked into the Al Fahidi Historic District since 2003, XVA's curators have a knack for ferreting out top-notch up-and-comers from around the Middle East. Works often express the artists' cultural identities and challenge viewers' preconceptions. It also shows at prestigious art fairs such as Art Basel and Art London. (☎ 04-353 5383; www.xvagallery.com; XVA Guesthouse, off Al Fahidi St; ⏱10am-6pm; M Al Fahidi)

Hindi Lane   STREET

3 Map p44, E2

The only place of worship for Dubai's sizeable Hindu community is the Shiva and Krishna Mandir, a temple complex just behind the Grand Mosque. From here you'll quickly reach a colourful alleyway that expats refer to as 'Hindi Lane' where vendors sell religious paraphernalia and offerings to take to the temples: baskets of fruit, garlands of flowers, gold-embossed holy images, sacred ash, sandalwood paste and packets of *bindis* (the little pendants Hindu women stick to their foreheads).
(off Ali bin Abi Talib St; M Al Fahidi, Al Ghubaiba)

Shindagha Historic District   NEIGHBOURHOOD

4 Map p44, D1

With a strategic location at the mouth of Dubai Creek, Shindagha was the Beverly Hills of Dubai in the first half of the 20th century. This is where the

Shops in Hindi Lane

ruling sheikhs, their families and the city elite lived in stately coral and gypsum homes wrapped around a central courtyard and cooled by wind towers. The entire area has been given a major facelift and is now a heritage district. (Shindagha Waterfront; M Al Ghubaiba)

Sheikh Saeed Al Maktoum House
MUSEUM

5 ◉ Map p44, D1

The grand courtyard house of Sheikh Saeed, the grandfather of current Dubai ruler Sheikh Mohammed bin Rashid, is the crown jewel of the restored Shindagha Historic District. Built in 1896, it served as Sheikh Saeed's private residence until his

death in 1958. Aside from being an architectural marvel, the building is now a museum of pre-oil times with an excellent collection of photographs of Dubai taken in the 1940s and '50s on the Creek, in the souqs and at traditional celebrations. (☎04-393 7139; Shindagha Historic District; adult/child Dh3/1; ◷8am-8.30pm Sat-Thu, 3-9.30pm Fri; M Al Ghubaiba)

Traditional Architecture Museum
MUSEUM

6 ◉ Map p44, D1

This magnificent courtyard house has seen stints as a residence, jail and police station. Today it houses a thorough exhibit on traditional Arab

Top Tip

Emirati Culture Demystified

Open doors, open minds: such is the motto of the **Sheikh Moham-med Centre for Cultural Under-standing** (Map p44, E2; ☎04-353 6666; www.cultures.ae; House 26, Al Mussalah Rd; tours Dh65, breakfast/lunch/dinner & brunch Dh80/90/100; ☻9am-5pm Sun-Thu, 9am-1pm Sat; Ⓜ︎Al Fahidi), an institution founded by Sheikh Mohammed in 1998 to build bridges between cultures and help visitors understand the tradi-tions and customs of the United Arab Emirates. Besides conducting guided tours of the Al Fahidi His-toric District and Jumeirah Mosque, the centre also hosts hugely popu-lar cultural breakfasts and lunches where you get a chance to meet, ask questions of and exchange ideas with Emiratis while savouring delicious home-cooked food. Early reservations advised.

architecture. This is the place to learn how those wind towers really work and why there are different dwelling types along the coast, in the moun-tains and in the desert. (Shindagha Historic District; admission free; ☻8am-8pm Mon-Sat, 8am-2pm Sun; Ⓜ︎Al Ghubaiba)

Camel Museum   MUSEUM

7 Map p44, D1

This exhibit raises the humble camel to celebrity status. It explains how and why the animals are held in such high regard in Arabian culture and depicts the historical importance of camels in the region and their prominence in Arabic literature. There are sections on camel racing and on the history of camels in region. (☎04-392 0368; Shindagha Historic District; admission free; ☻8am-2pm Sun-Thu; Ⓜ︎Al Ghubaiba)

Heritage Village   MUSEUM

8 Map p44, E1

This outdoor museum is a well-meaning attempt at recreating a village from pre-oil times and features various styles of houses (coastal and mountain), a small souq, historic exhibits and crafts stations. From October to April, there are occasion-ally activities and demonstrations, although most of the time the place seems sadly neglected. (Shindagha Historic District; admission free; ☻8.30am-10.30pm Sat-Thu, 4.30pm-10.30pm Fri; Ⓜ︎Al Ghubaiba)

Diving Village   MUSEUM

9 ◉ Map p44, E1

At this outdoor museum, you can delve into Dubai's maritime history and learn about the harsh reali-ties of life as a pearl diver and the importance of diving and trading to the region. There's a smattering of old boats to help visitors take a step back in time. (☎04-393 7139; Shindagha Historic District; admission free; ☻8.30am-10pm Sat-Thu, 3.30-10pm Sun; Ⓜ︎Al Ghubaiba)

Big Bus Dubai

BUS TOUR

10 ⊙ Map p44, C8

These 'hop-on, hop-off' city tours aboard open-topped double-decker buses are a good way for Dubai first-timers to get their bearing. Buses run on three interlinking routes, stopping at major malls, beaches and landmarks and include taped commentary in 12 languages and such extras as a souq walking tour or a dhow minicruise. Tickets are sold online, on the bus or at hotels. There's also a nonstop 2¾-hour Night Tour (adult/child Dh145/75). (☑04-340 7709; www.bigbustours.com; 24hr ticket adult/child Dh240/100, 48hr Dh295/130)

Wonder Bus Tours

BOAT TOUR

11 ⊙ Map p44, D4

These unusual sightseeing tours have you boarding the bright yellow amphibious Wonder Bus at the BurJuman Centre, driving down to the Creek, plunging into the water, cruising past historic Bur Dubai and Deira and returning to the shopping mall, all within the space of one hour. (☑04-359 5656; http://wonderbusdubai.net; ground fl, BurJuman Centre; adult/child 3-11yr Dh160/115; ⊙several times daily; Ⓜ BurJuman)

Za'abeel Park

PARK

12 ⊙ Map p44, A5

This sprawling park is hugely popular with families and filled with activity zones, including a pretty lake with cascades and a restaurant as well as interactive themed areas such as a Technology Zone, a Barcode Garden, an Alternative Energy Zone and a Space Maze. Views are great from the 45m-high Panoramic Tower. (☑04-325 9988; Gate 1, off Sheikh Khalifa bin Zayed Rd; admission Dh5; ⊙8am-10pm Sun-Wed, to 11pm Thu-Sat; ♿ Ⓜ Al Jafiliya)

Eating

Qbara

MIDDLE EASTERN $$$

Qbara (see 27 🔀 Map p44, C8) gets our vote for most beautiful restaurant in Dubai. Think dark, mysterious and sensuous with a 10m-long bar leading to the circular dining room punctuated with a huge glass-bubble chandelier. The bar is backed by a wall carved with Islamic motifs reaching all the way to the upstairs lounge. The innovative modern Arabian cuisine can easily compete with the stunning decor. (☑04-709 2500; www.qbara.ae; Wafi Fort Complex, near 13th & 28th Sts; mains Dh90-250; ⊙6pm-1am; Ⓜ Dubai Healthcare City)

Jaffer Bhai's

INDIAN $

13 🔀 Map p44, D5

Jaffer Bhai, the self-crowned 'biryani king of Mumbai', now feeds his soulful fare to adoring crowds in this modern Karama eatery decorated with a timeline of his career. The chicken biryani gets tops marks and the mutton *nihari* (the house speciality) is quite good as well, although perhaps a bit oily. Finish up with *maharani rabdi,* the Indian spin on crème brûlée. (☑04-342 6467;

Za'abeel Rd; mains Dh19-43; ⊘noon-midnight Sat-Thu, from 1pm Fri; Ⓜ️ADCB)

Special Ostadi
IRANIAN $

14 Map p44, D3

Everybody feels like family at this been-here-forever (since 1978 to be precise) spit-and-sawdust eatery presided over by the magnificently mustachioed Mohammed. Amid walls plastered with photographs of happy guests, a fleet of swift servers brings out heaping plates of rice and kebabs into a dining room humming with

---

Top Tip

Hitting 'Old Dubai's Food Trail

For a mouthwatering immersion into Bur Dubai's polyethnic food and culture, book a culinary walking tour with local blogger and foodie extraordinaire Arva Ahmed, founder of **Frying Pan Adventures** (www.fryingpanadventures.com; tours Dh280-520). Wandering around the district's bewildering tangle of lanes, you'll taste exotic nibbles from such far-flung locales as India, Iran, Yemen, Nepal, Morocco and Ethiopia at five or six hidden gems. En route Arva showers you with fascinating tidbits about the food, the restaurant and the culture. Some of her tours also explore Deira across the Creek. Check the website for the schedule and the booking function.

---

chatter and laughter. (📞04-397 1469; Al Musallah Rd; mains Dh20-40; ⊘noon-4pm Sat-Thu, 6.30pm-1am daily; Ⓜ️Al Fahidi)

Kan Zaman
MIDDLE EASTERN $

15 Map p44, E1

This traditional Creekside hangout is perfect for watching the sunset over a juice and mezze, but to see it at its bustling best you need to come later in the evening when *sheesha* (water pipe) aficionados invade to relax with a view of the dhows heading out to sea. It's near Al Shindagha Tunnel. (📞04-393 9913; Shindagha Historic District; appetizers Dh10-36, grills Dh35-59, sheesha Dh30; ⊘5pm-2am; Ⓜ️Al Ghubaiba)

Tomo
JAPANESE $$$

Visiting celebs aren't the only ones who love this gorgeously formal lair (see 27 Ⓖ Map p44, C8), where Chitoshi Takahashi serves top Japanese cuisine. No gimmicky fusion here, just perfect superfresh cuts of sushi and sashimi, delectable Wagyu beef, feathery tempura and other treasured morsels served on the 17th floor of the Raffles hotel. Snag a table on the 360° terrace with the entire city glittering below. (📞04-357 7888; www.tomo.ae; Wafi City, Raffles hotel; mains Dh70-550; ⊘12.30-3.30pm & 6.30pm-1am; 📶; Ⓜ️Dubai Healthcare City)

Arabian Tea House
CAFE $

16 Map p44, E2

A grand old tree, white wicker chairs, turquoise benches and billowing flowers create a sun-dappled refuge

Coffee Museum (p43), Al Fahidi Historic District

in the courtyard of an old pearl merchant's house. The food is respectable cafe fare – salads, sandwiches, quiches – but it's the vast selection of quality teas that makes this place so special. For a local treat, try the Arabian breakfast. (☑04-353 5071; Al Fahidi St; mains Dh30-45; ☺7am-11pm; Ⓜ Al Fahidi)

Picante   PORTUGUESE $$

17 ✕ Map p44, D3

Picante is decked out in orange and blue, the dominant colours of the bluffs and the sea of the Algarve beaches on the south coast of Portugal whose cuisine it celebrates. Typical dishes include *bacalhau* (salt cod fillet), *estufado* (chicken stew) and *pastel de nata* (egg custard) for dessert. (☑04-397 7444; www.picantedubai.com; Four Points by Sheraton Bur Dubai, Khalid bin al Walid Rd; mains Dh70-160; ☺lunch & dinner; 🛜; Ⓜ Al Fahidi)

Jambo's Grill   EAST AFRICAN $$

18 ✕ Map p44, D5

Study the colourful mural of East Africa while taking your taste buds on a safari around Kenya and Tanzania at this upbeat Karama eatery. This is the place to try *mishkaki*, super-tender chunks of beef served with two chutneys and a fiery hot sauce; the co-conut-based *kuku paka* roast chicken curry; and the intensely spiced prawn *pili-pili* (chilli sauce). Nice mocktails

Local Life

Bacchanalian Boating

A delightful way to experience the magic of 'Old Dubai' is on a Creek dinner cruise. Feed tummy and soul as you float past historic waterfront houses, sparkling high-rises, jutting wind towers and dhows bound for Iran. Dining rooms are air-conditioned and alcohol is served. **Bateaux Dubai** (Map p44, E3; ☑04-814 5553; www.bateauxdubai.com; Al Seef Rd, next to Rulers Court, Bur Dubai waterfront; per person 2½hr dinner cruise Dh400; ☺8.30-11pm; Ⓜ Al Fahidi) is a good choice, serving four-course à la carte feasts aboard a stylish contemporary boat with panoramic windows, linen-draped tables and live music.

too. (☑04-358 3583; www.jambosgrill.com; Za'abeel Rd; mains Dh18-109; ☺noon-3pm & 7pm-midnight Tue-Thu, Sat & Sun, 1-4pm & 7pm-midnight Fri; Ⓜ ADCB)

Antique Bazaar   INDIAN $$

19 Map p44, D3

Resembling an exotic Mogul palace, Antique Bazaar's decor is sumptuously ornate with carved-wood seats, ivory-inset tables and richly patterned fabrics. Thumbs up to the *machli mirch ka salan* (fish with coconut, tamarind and curry) and the *gosht awadhi biryani* (rice with lamb, saffron and nuts). At dinnertime, a music and dance show competes with the food for your attention. (☑04-397 7444; Four Points by Sheraton Bur Dubai, Khalid bin al Waleed Rd; mains Dh42-90; ☺lunch & dinner; 🛜; Ⓜ Al Fahidi)

XVA Café   CAFE $

Tucked into the historic Al Fahidi district, this cultured courtyard cafe (see 2 ◉ Map p44, E2) set within the eponymous boutique hotel and gallery puts the emphasis on meat-free fare such as eggplant burgers, burghul salad and *morjardara* (rice topped with sauteed veggies and yogurt). The mint lemonade is a great energy booster on a hot day. (☑04-353 5383; www.xvahotel.com/cafe; off Al Fahidi St; mains Dh20-35; ☺9am-7pm Sat-Thu, 10am-5pm Fri Nov-Apr; 🖋; Ⓜ Al Fahidi)

Sind Punjab   INDIAN $

20 ✖ Map p44, D2

Like a fine wine, some restaurants only get better over time and such is the case with Sind Punjab, the first family eatery to open in Meena Bazaar in 1977. Since then, the low-frills eatery has garnered a feverishly loyal following for its finger-lickin' butter chicken and *dal makhani* (a rich lentil and kidney bean stew). (☑04-352 5058; Bukaz Bldg, Meena Bazaar, Al Esbij St; mains Dh11-35; ☺8am-1.30pm; Ⓜ Al Fahidi, Al Ghubaiba)

Govinda's   VEGETARIAN $

21 ✖ Map p44, D4

Jains run this super friendly, super healthy vegetarian Indian restaurant where the cooking is rich in character even though the chefs shun oil, onion and garlic. Dishes to try include the velvety *paneer makhanwala* (butter paneer) and the rich *dal makhani*. Do save room for the homemade Tru Frut natural ice cream from the attached parlour. Also tops for mocktails. (☎04-396 0088; www.govindasdubai.com; 4A St; mains Dh22-35; ☉lunch & dinner Sat-Thu; 🍴; MBurJuman)

Lemongrass
THAI **$**

22 Map p44, B6

Lemongrass' soothing mango-and-lime-coloured dining room is an ideal backdrop for brightly flavoured cooking that spans the arc from pad thai (nicely presented in an omelette wrapper) to curries with a marvellous depth of flavour. If you like spicy, say so; the kitchen can be shy with the heat. Located next to Lamcy Plaza. (☎04-334 2325; www.lemongrassrestaurants.com; ground fl, Bu Haleeba Bldg; mains Dh26-69; ☉noon-11.30pm; MOud Metha)

Bait Al Wakeel
ARABIAN **$$**

23 Map p44, D1

Teeming with tourists lured by the romantic Creekside setting, this restaurant occupies one of Dubai's oldest buildings (from 1935) and has a great wooden dining deck that used to be a boat landing. Come for coffee, juice or mezze and enjoy the view. Secret tip: for an even better perspective, head up to the roof via the stairs at the back of the restaurant. (☎04-353 0530; Bur Dubai Souq, waterfront; mezze Dh12-30, mains Dh35-120; ☉noon-11pm; MAl Ghubaiba)

Drinking

People by Crystal
CLUB

On the two top floors of the pyramid-shaped Raffles, this see-and-be-seen club (see 27 ☻ Map p44, C8) boasts made-to-impress decor, panoramic city views and world-class DJs. There are lots of nooks and lounges for quiet tête-à-têtes if you need a break from the dance floor. (☎050-297 2097; www.dubai.raffles.com; Raffles Dubai, Sheikh Rashid Rd; ☉11pm-3am Thu-Sat; MDubai Healthcare City)

George & Dragon
PUB

24 ☻ Map p44, D1

Keeping barflies boozy for over 15 years, this quintessential British dive comes with the requisite dart board, pool table, greasy fish and chips, cheap beer and a painted window of St George jousting with the dragon. Inside the Ambassador, Dubai's oldest hotel (since 1971), it's fun and full of character(s) but perhaps not the ideal place for date night. (☎04-393 9444; Meena Bazaar, Al Falah Rd; ☉7pm-3am; MAl Ghubaiba)

Rock Bottom Café
PUB

25 ☻ Map p44, D4

This been-here-forever place has a '70s-era American roadhouse feel, with a cover band blaring out Top-40 hits and a DJ filling in the breaks with gusto. By day it's a regular cafe serving Tex-Mex, but with a mob of friends and a bottle of tequila gone, it's the quintessential ending to a rollickin' night on the town. (☑04-396 3888; Regent Palace Hotel, Sheikh Khalifa bin Zayed Rd; ⊘noon-3am; 🛜; MBurJuman)

Entertainment

Music Room
LIVE MUSIC

26 ⭐ Map p44, C3

Arab hip-hop queen Malikah and English metal band Salem are among the many artists who've played gigs at Dubai's best place for indie and alt-sounds from local, regional and international talent. Great for dipping into

Local Life
Desert Safaris

There's nothing like experiencing the desert, which is why residents frequently make an effort to get out of the city and onto the emirate's sand-swept roads. Whether it's for a drive for some camel-spotting, a weekend of camping or a few days relaxing at a dreamy resort, it's amazing how mind-clearing desert time can be.

For travellers on short trips to Dubai, an organised 4WD desert safari is the most popular way to experience the Arabian sands. Several reliable tour companies, including long-established **Arabian Adventures** (☑04-303 4888; www. arabian-adventures.com; sundowner adult/child Dh330/295), offer a wide range of tours and excursions.

the local music scene, it's the kind of spot that appeals to music aficionados who keep attitude to a minimum. (☑04-359 8888; www.themusicroomdubai. com; Majestic Hotel, Al Mankhool Rd; ⊘8pm-3am; MAl Fahidi)

Shopping

Wafi Mall
SHOPPING MALL

27 🔒 Map p44, C8

At the heart of Wafi City, a hotel, retail and residential complex designed in the style of ancient Egypt, is one of Dubai's older but architecturally most stunning malls. Alas, eclipsed by bigger and more central ones, it's often sadly deserted. Its biggest eyecatchers are the stained-glass pyramids and a vast dome. In the basement, the Souq Khan Murjan sells crafts from around the Arabian world and was modelled after the original Baghdad bazaar. (☑04-324 4555; www.wafi.com; Sheikh Rashid & Oud Metha Rds; ⊘10am-10pm Sat-Wed, to midnight Thu & Fri; MDubai Healthcare City)

BurJuman
SHOPPING MALL

28 🔒 Map p44, D4

This high-end mall was in the process of large-scale remodelling at the time we visited. Once completed, it will boast a new 14-screen multiplex cinema, an expanded food court and a vast Carrefour supermarket branch in addition to an eclectic mix of stores from high-street chains to couture brands. (☑04-352 0222; www.

Interior of Wafi Mall

burjuman.com; Sheikh Khalifa bin Zayed Rd;
⏱10am-10pm Sat-Wed, to 11pm Thu & Fri; 📶;
Ⓜ BurJuman)

Saks Fifth Avenue   FASHION

Founded in 1898 in New York City, the
Dubai branch of this luxury department store (see 28 Ⓐ Map p44, D4) has
kept label-loving Dubai residents and
visitors looking good for over a decade.
Racks brim with both classic designers
such as Balmain and Cerruti as well
as the latest shooting stars, including
some regional contenders such as Fei-
ruza Mudessir's label Finchitua. (☎04-
501 2700; www.saksme.com; BurJuman Mall,
Sheikh Khalifa bin Zayed Rd; ⏱10am-10pm
Sun-Wed, to 11pm Thu & Fri; Ⓜ BurJuman)

Bateel   FOOD

Old-style traditional Arabian hospitality meant dates and camel milk.
Now Emiratis offer their guests Bateel's (see 28 Ⓐ Map p44, D4) scrumptious
date chocolates and truffles, made
using European chocolate-making
techniques. Staff are happy to give
you a sample before you buy. Check
the website for additional branches,
and if you fancy a date cake or
pastry, check out Cafe Bateel on the
same level. (☎04-359 7932; www.bateel.
com; BurJuman Mall, Sheikh Khalifa bin
Zayed Rd; ⏱10am-10pm Sun-Wed, to 11pm
Thu & Fri; Ⓜ BurJuman)

Fabindia

FASHION

29 🔒 Map p44, B2

In business since 1950, Fabindia is one of India's biggest retail chains and sells mostly products made by Indian villagers using traditional skills and techniques. There's a huge selection of fashion, furnishings and handicrafts, including colourful *kurtis* (tunics), elegant shawls, patterned silk cushions and organic teas and chutneys, all sold at very reasonable prices. It's near the EPPCO petrol station. (☑04-398 9633; www.fabindia.com; Al Mankhool Rd; ◷10am-10pm Sat-Thu, 4-10pm Fri; Ⓜ ADCB)

Sun & Sand Sports Factory Outlet

SPORTING GOODS

30 🔒 Map p44, D3

This is the factory outlet branch of one of the biggest sporting goods retailers in the region with a store-room jam-packed with shoes, rackets, jackets and more from major international brands. Prices tend to be a bit lower than usual, but it's the big selection that gives this place an additional edge. (☑04-351 6222; www.sunandsandsports.com; Khalid bin al Waleed Rd, near 18th St; ◷10am-10pm; Ⓜ BurJuman)

Understand

A Primer on Bargaining

In malls and most stores prices are fixed, but in souqs and outdoor markets, it pays to know some bargaining basics.

▶ Compare prices at a few shops or stalls so you get an idea of what things cost and how much you're willing to pay.

▶ When you're interested in buying an item, don't show too much enthusiasm or you'll never get the price down.

▶ Start below the price you wish to pay so you have room to compromise – but don't quote too low or risk that the vendor feels insulted. A good rule of thumb is to cut the first suggested price in half and go from there. Expect to finish up with a discount of 20% to 30%.

▶ If you intend to buy more than one item, use this as a bargaining chip – the more you buy, the better the discount.

▶ Take your time and stay relaxed. You can come away with an enjoyable experience whether you end up with a bargain or not.

▶ If negotiations aren't going to plan, simply smile and say goodbye – often the vendor will follow and suggest a compromise price.

Ajmal
PERFUME

The place for traditional Arabian *attars* (perfumes), Ajmal (see 28 ⓐ Map p44, D4) custom blends its earthy scents and pours them into fancy gold- or jewel-encrusted bottles. These aren't frilly French colognes – they're woody and pungent perfumes. Ask for the signature scent 'Ajmal', based on white musk and jasmine. Other branches are in Deira City Centre, Mall of the Emirates and Dubai Mall. (☎04-351 5505; www.ajmalperfume.com; BurJuman Mall, Sheikh Khalifa bin Zayed Rd; ☺10am-10pm Sat-Wed, to 11pm Thu & Fri; Ⓜ BurJuman)

Computer Plaza @ Al Ain Centre
ELECTRONICS

31 ⓐ Map p44, D3

Jam-packed with small shops selling every kind of software, hardware and accessory for PCs, this computer and electronics mall also has a good range of digital cameras and mobile phones. On the ground floor a handful of fast-food outlets and an ice cream counter keep tummy rumblings in check. It's next to Spinneys. (☎04-352 6663; www.alaincentre.com; Al Mankhool Rd; ☺10am-10pm Sat-Thu, 2-10pm Fri; Ⓜ Al Fahidi)

Karama Market
SHOPPING AREA

32 ⓐ Map p44, C5

A visually unappealing concrete souq, Karama's bustling backstreet shopping area is crammed with stores selling handicrafts and souvenirs. Vendors may offer to take you to 'secret rooms' in the back of the building that are crammed with knock-off designer bags and watches.

Quality varies, so it pays to have a keen eye and to know what the originals look like. Prices are low, but bargaining lowers them further. (18B St; Ⓜ ADCB)

Silk Wonders
SOUVENIRS

33 ⓐ Map p44, E2

Near the Dubai Museum, this is one of several pick-and-mix stores filled with inexpensive stuff to bring the folks back home. Max out your luggage allowance with shawls, perfumes, embroidered clutches, sequined bedspreads and pillows, woven silk-and-wool rugs, ornaments from India, Iranian carved boxes and plenty of other neat trinkets. (☎04-351 3251; www.silkwonder.com; Atheryat Mall, Al Fahidi St; Ⓜ Al Fahidi)

Royal Saffron
SPICES

34 ⓐ Map p44, E2

This tiny shop tucked into the quiet lanes of the Al Fahidi Historic District is a photogenic find. It's crammed full of spices such as cloves, cardamom and cinnamon, plus fragrant oils, dried fruits and nuts, frankincense from Somalia and Oman, henna hair dye – and quirky salt and pepper sheikh and sheikhas. (Al Fahidi Historic District; Ⓜ Al Fahidi)

Explore

Jumeirah & Around

Before there was Dubai Marina and Downtown Dubai, everybody went to Jumeirah to realise their Dubai dreams. It's the emirate's answer to Bondi or Malibu, with great beaches, boutique shopping, copious medi-spas and beauty clinics, and a mix of Mercedes and expensive 4WDs in villa driveways. Jumeirah rubs up against vibrant Satwa, which teems with bustling budget restaurants.

JOHN KELLERMAN / ALAMY ©

The Sights in a Day

☀ Cruise into the day with an early-morning stroll on the beach, then aim for a perfect balance of spirituality and architecture at the **Jumeirah Mosque** (p62). Refuel with coffee or juice at the expat darling, **Lime Tree Cafe** (p64).

☀ If it's not too hot, embark on a spot of boutique hopping down Jumeirah Rd, checking out extravagant designer threads in such local lairs as **S*uce** (p64) and **O-Concept** (p64) or at high-end chains in the **Mercato Mall** (p65), with its stunning Italianate architectural detail. For a late lunch, pop into the Town Centre next door for a taste of traditional Emirati cuisine at **Al Fanar** (p62), then spend the rest of the afternoon on the beach.

☾ A classic dinner spot around here is **Ravi** (p62), an earthy been-here-forever eatery serving some of the best Indian and Pakistani food in town. Head back to the shore for after-dinner drinks at **Sho Cho** (p64) in the Dubai Marine Beach Resort, then mingle with hotties on the dance floor at **Boudoir** (p64).

 Best of Dubai

Eating
Ravi (p62)
Samad Al Iraqi (p62)
Al Fanar (p62)

Shopping
S*uce (p64)
O-Concept (p64)

Getting There

Ⓜ **Metro** Jumeirah is not directly served by metro. The closest stops are World Trade Centre, Emirates Tower, Financial Centre and Burj Khalifa/Dubai Mall, all on the Red Line. From here you'll need to catch a taxi to your final destination.

🚌 **Bus** Buses 8, 88 and X28 travel the entire length of Jumeira Rd down to the Burj Al Arab.

A　　　B　　　C　　　D

THE GULF

1

0 ─────── 500 m
0 ─────── 0.25 miles

For reviews see	
◉ Sights	p62
✗ Eating	p62
◐ Drinking	p64
⬤ Shopping	p64

2

43A

✗5

75A　75A

Jumeirah Rd

8A

6D

14A

41A

◀✗2

7 ✗✗4

◐12

69A

59A

10D

45A

51

16C

41A

20B

3

75B

79　71B

26C

JUMEIRAH 1

28B

69B　65B

Al Wasl Rd

2C

32C

◀◐13

2D　81　79　75

63

4

Al Satwa Rd

Al Safa St

57A

5

E   F   G   H

1

8 🚻
🚻 9

Jumeirah Open
Beach

Jumeirah Rd

5   3

🅿 10
15B   11   4A   Jumeirah
Mosque
1 🕌
2B

2

35A

2D
6C
27B
25A
2C
6B
21A

10A

2A

24A

6B
10B
16A
24B

11
17B

10C

16B
20A
24D
35
39B
29
33
25B
24C
2
3
21B
27A

2A   17A
6A

2A   7A

3

Al Wasl Rd

Al Hudhaiba Rd

8A

12A

🆑 6

3C

Satwa
Roundabout

2B
43A
49
45
41
6B
31
29
8B
12B
25
23
21
16B
17B
20A
12A
14B
16A   18A

4

Al Satwa Rd

3 🆑
6A

6B
10B
8A
6C
8C
13A
12A

19
18B
20A
SATWA

22A

18A
20B
21
22B
30A

Al Dhiyafah St

Al Dhiyafah St

5

Sights

Jumeirah Mosque
MOSQUE

1 ◎ Map p60, F2

Snowy-white and intricately detailed, Jumeirah is not only one of Dubai's most beautiful mosques, but it is also the only one open to non-Muslims during one-hour guided tours operated by the Sheikh Mohammed Centre for Cultural Understanding (p48). All tours conclude with a Q&A session where you are free to ask any question about Islamic religion and culture. There's no need to prebook. Modest dress is preferred but traditional clothing may be borrowed for free before entering the mosque. Cameras are allowed. (☏04-353 6666; www. cultures.ae; Jumeirah Rd; tours Dh10; ☉tours 10-11.15am Sat-Thu; Ⓜ Emirates Towers, World Trade Centre)

Top Tip

Jumeirah Beaches

Jumeirah is famous for its beaches, but two of its most popular stretches of sand are actually closed for the foreseeable future. Jumeirah Open Beach, near the Jumeirah Mosque, is undergoing private development, while Jumeirah Beach Park is closed because of the construction of the Dubai Canal.

Eating

Samad Al Iraqi
IRAQI $$

2 ✕ Map p60, A2

This huge restaurant with decor evocative of ancient Iraq enjoys an especially loyal local following because of its excellent *masgouf* – wood-fire grilled fish that's considered Iraq's national dish. There are lots of other tempting stews and grills, many served with hot *tanour* bread or biryani rice. (☏04-342 7887; http://samadaliraqi restaurant.com; Jumeirah Beach Park Plaza, Jumeirah 2; mains Dh50-85; ☉9am-12.30am Sat-Thu, 1pm-1.30am Fri; Ⓜ Business Bay)

Ravi
PAKISTANI $

3 ✕ Map p60, H4

Everyone from cabbies to five-star chefs flock to this original branch of the legendary Pakistani eatery (dating from 1978) where you eat like a prince and pay like a pauper. Possibly home to the best butter chicken in town, it's also worth loosening that belt for helpings of spicy curries, grilled meats, creamy *dal* (lentils) and fresh naan. (☏04-331 5353; Al Satwa Rd, Satwa; mains Dh8-25; ☉5am-2.30am; Ⓜ World Trade Centre)

Al Fanar
EMIRATI $$

4 ✕ Map p60, A2

Al Fanar lays on the old-timey Emirati theme pretty thick with a Land Rover parked outside, a reed ceiling and waiters dressed in traditional garb. Make your selection with the help of a

SYLVAIN SONNET / GETTY IMAGES ©

Jumeirah Mosque

picture menu depicting such dishes as *biryani laham* (rice with lamb), *maleh nashef* (salted fish in tomato sauce) and *thereed deyay* (chicken stew with Arabian bread). (☎04-344 2141; www.alfanarrestaurant.com; Town Centre mall, Jumeirah Rd, Jumeirah 1; mains Dh45-75; ☺8.30am-11.30pm; Ⓜ Burj Khalifa/Dubai Mall)

Comptoir 102   MACROBIOTIC $$

5 🍽 Map p60, D2

In a pretty villa with a quiet patio out the back, this concept cafe comes attached to a concept boutique selling beautiful things for home and hearth. The daily changing menu rides the local-organic-seasonal wave and eschews gluten, sugar and dairy. There's also a big selection of super

healthy juices, smoothies and desserts. It's opposite Beach Centre mall. (☎04-385 4555; www.comptoir102.com; Jumeirah Rd 102, Jumeirah 1; mains Dh55-65, 3-course meal Dh90; ☺8am-11pm; Ⓜ Emirates Towers)

Al Mallah   LEBANESE $

6 🍽 Map p60, H3

Serving some of the most delicious shwarmas around, along with excellent other Lebanese staples, this funky eatery with shaded outdoor seating is a great choice for a quick snack and a fresh juice (served in three sizes). It's on Al Diyafah, one of Dubai's most pleasant and liveliest walking streets. (☎04-398 4723; Al Dhiyafah St, Satwa; sandwiches Dh6-12, mains Dh14-60; ☺6am-4am Sat-Thu, noon-4am Fri; Ⓜ World Trade Centre, Al Jafiliya)

Mama Tani
EMIRATI **$**

7 Map p60, A2

Khameer is a traditional Emirati bread normally eaten at breakfast but served all day at this cheerful cafe decorated with woven-reed discs called *sarrouds*. You can have it plain or like a sandwich stuffed with your choice of sweet or savoury ingredients such as feta, avocado, saffron cream, figs, mint or rose petals. (☑04-385 4437; www.mama tani.com; upstairs, Town Centre mall, Jumeirah Rd, Jumeirah 1; khameer Dh11-26; ☺8am-10pm; 🛜📶; Ⓜ Burj Khalifa/Dubai Mall)

Drinking

Sho Cho
BAR, CLUB

8 Map p60, F1

The cool minimalist interior, with its blue lights and wall-mounted fish tanks, may draw you in, but the beach-

---

Local Life
'Liming' with the Locals

The comfy Euro-style **Lime Tree Cafe** (Map p60, F2; ☑04-325 6325; www.thelimetreecafe.com; Jumeirah Rd, Jumeirah 1; mains Dh20-55; ☺8am-6pm; 🛜; Ⓜ World Trade Centre) is a Western expat favourite famous for its cakes (especially the carrot cake), delicious sandwiches (stuffed into their homemade Turkish pide), roast chicken and pasta dishes. Settle down with your iPad or keep it old-school with a newspaper and enjoy some downtime in a cosy setting.

---

side deck is the place to be. Take in the laid-back vibe as the cool ocean breezes blow and the DJ's soundtrack competes with the crashing waves. (☑04-346 1111; www.sho-cho.com; Dubai Marine Beach Resort & Spa, Jumeirah Rd, Jumeirah 1; ☺7pm-3am Sun-Fri; Ⓜ World Trade Centre, Emirates Towers)

Boudoir
CLUB

9 Map p60, F1

High on the glam-o-meter, Boudoir has been around the block but isn't showing its age – and neither are its fashionable patrons. Sounds run the gamut from house to hip-hop to *desi* (Bollywood) nights. (☑050-375 7377; www.boudoirdubai. com; Dubai Marine Beach Resort & Spa, Jumeirah Rd; ☺9pm-3am; Ⓜ World Trade Centre)

Shopping

S*uce
FASHION

10 Map p60, E2

Plain and simple they are not, the clothes and accessories at S*uce (pronounced 'sauce'), a pioneer in Dubai's growing lifestyle fashion scene. Join fashionistas picking through international designers you probably won't find on your high street back home (eg India's Anouk Grewal, Lebanon's Vanina). (☑04-344 7270; http://shopatsauce.com; Village Mall, Jumeirah Beach Rd; ☺10am-10pm Sat-Thu, 4-10pm Fri; Ⓜ Emirates Towers)

O-Concept
FASHION & ACCESSORIES

11 Map p60, F2

This Emirati-owned urban boutique-cum-cafe with shiny concrete floors

Understand
Dubai Canal

One of the city's latest megaprojects is the construction of the Dubai Canal, a 3km extension of the Dubai Creek all the way to the Arabian Gulf. The broad waterway originally ran 15km from its mouth in Deira and Bur Dubai down to the Ras Al Khor Wildlife Sanctuary; it was first extended by 2.2km to the new Business Bay district in 2007.

In December 2013, construction kicked off on the new canal. It's planned course will meander from Business Bay below Sheikh Zayed Road, through Safa Park and then spill into the sea at Jumeirah Beach. As envisioned, it will add 6km of waterfront lined by a shopping mall, hotels, restaurants, cafes, residences, marinas, a public beach, a jogging track and other public spaces. Several bridges will link the banks. The projected completion date is 2017. Until then, there will be numerous traffic diversions, plus the closing of Jumeirah Beach Park and sections of Safa Park.

and ducts wrapped in gold foil is a routine stop for fashionistas in search of up-to-the-second T-shirts, dresses, jeans and other fashions by a changing roster of young international labels such as Australia's Deadly Companions or Finland's Shine by Sophia. It's near Jumeirah Mosque. (☎04-345 5557; www.oconcept.ae; Al Hudheiba Rd; ⊙10am-10pm; Ⓜ World Trade Center)

Mercato Mall SHOPPING MALL
12 🔒 Map p60, B3

With 140 stores, Mercato may be small by Dubai standards but it's distinguished by attractive architecture that's a fantasy blend of a European train station and an Italian Renaissance village. Think vaulted glass roof, brick arches, a giant clock and a cafe-lined central 'square' called Piazza Grande. Retail-wise, you'll find upscale international brands and a Spinney's supermarket. (☎04-344 4161; www.mercatoshoppingmall.com; Jumeirah Rd, Jumeirah 1; ⊙10am-10pm; Ⓜ Financial Centre, Burj Khalifa/Dubai Mall)

Galleria Mall SHOPPING MALL
13 🔒 Map p60, A4

This chic concept minimall is a laid-back alternative to the big-mall craziness. Pick up outdoor gear at Adventure HQ, 24-carat-gold shower gel at Stenders or a stylish outfit for your preteen at local designer Saucette, then wrap up with a healthy meal at South African cafe Tashas or gooey cakes at Home Bakery. It's next to Jumeirah Post Office. (www.thegalleria.ae; Al Wasl Rd, near 13th St; ⊙10am-10pm Sat-Wed, to midnight Thu & Fri; Ⓜ Burj Khalifa/Dubai Mall)

Explore

Burj Al Arab & Madinat Jumeirah

The iconic Burj Al Arab is the shining star of this beautiful stretch of coast, also home to Madinat Jumeirah, a canal-laced 'Arabian Venice' complete with hotels, cafes and boutiques. More great shopping awaits inland at the Mall of the Emirates, which shelters the deliciously surreal Ski Dubai indoor ski park. Art aficionados, meanwhile, gravitate to gritty Al Quoz and its galleries.

The Sights in a Day

☼ Greet the day with strong java and a healthy breakfast at **Tom & Serg** (p72), an ultrahip industrial loft cafe, before perusing the latest in Middle Eastern art on a gallery hop around the **Alserkal Avenue** (p73) warehouse complex in the industrial district of Al Quoz.

☼ Cab or metro it to the **Mall of the Emirates** (p76) to spend the hottest part of the day picking out some chic new threads and dipping into the 'Alps in the Desert' at **Ski Dubai** (p76). Time to make a beeline to **Madinat Jumeirah** (p68) for a spot of souvenir shopping at **Souk Madinat Jumeirah** (p68), followed by a relaxing *abra* (wooden ferry) ride around this charming Arabian-style resort.

☾ With the most magical time of day coming up, stake out a spot at **360°** (p78) and put your digicam into overdrive as the sun sinks into the horizon while the **Burj Al Arab** (p70) cuts its usual elegant figure. For a different perspective of the same, book ahead for seafood dinner at **Pierchic** (p77), perhaps followed by a nightcap at the romantic **Bahri Bar** (p79) or a spin on the dance floor of **Pacha Ibiza Dubai** (p79).

For a local's day in Burj Al Arab & Madinat Jumeirah, see p72.

Top Sights

Madinat Jumeirah (p68)

Burj Al Arab (p70)

◯ Local Life

Gallery Hopping around Al Quoz (p72)

♥ Best of Dubai

Eating

Pierchic (p77)

Pai Thai (p77)

Tom & Serg (p72)

Drinking

360° (p78)

Bahri Bar (p79)

Mazology (p79)

Beaches

Kite Beach (p76)

Sunset Beach (p71)

Getting There

Ⓜ **Metro** The closest metro stop to the Burj Al Arab and Madinat Jumeirah is Mall of the Emirates. For Al Quoz or Kite Beach, get off at Noor Bank. You'll need a taxi to get to your final destination.

Top Sights
Madinat Jumeirah

One of Dubai's most attractive recent developments, Madinat Jumeirah is a contemporary interpretation of a traditional Arab village, complete with a souq, palm-fringed waterways and desert-coloured hotels and villas festooned with wind towers. It's especially enchanting at night when the gardens and grounds are romantically lit and the Burj Al Arab gleams in the background. At the heart of the complex lies Souk Madinat Jumeirah, a mazelike bazaar with shops lining wood-framed walkways.

👁 Map p74, B3

www.jumeirah.com

Al Sufouh Rd, Umm Suqeim

Ⓜ Mall of the Emirates

Madinat Jumeirah

Don't Miss

Souk Madinat Jumeirah

Although tourist-geared, this handsome souq is not a bad place for picking up souvenirs. Plenty of charming cafes, bars and restaurants line the waterfront, while on Saturday mornings an organic farmers market displays farm-fresh bounty in one of its courtyards (December to May).

Abra Cruising

Explore Madinat's 4km-long network of winding waterways on a leisurely 20-minute **tour** (adult/child Dh75/40) aboard an *abra*, a traditional wooden boat. The desert seems far away as you glide past enchanting gardens of billowing bougainvillea, bushy banana trees and soaring palms, all set against the dramatic Burj Al Arab backdrop. Tours leave from the Souk Madinat waterfront (near the Left Bank bar). No reservations are necessary.

Friday Brunch

Friday brunch is a time-honoured tradition, especially among Western expats. The two Madinat hotels **Al Qasr** (☑04-366 6730; soft drinks/alcohol/champagne Dh475/575/795; ⊘12.30-4pm Fri) and **Mina A' Salam** (☑04-366 6730; without/with alcohol Dh425/525; ⊘12.30-4pm Fri; 🛝) put on some of the most impressive spreads in town. Both feature an unbelievable cornucopia of delectables – roast lamb, sushi, cooked-to-order seafood, foie gras, beautiful salads, mezze, all sorts of hot dishes, plus cheese and dessert rooms. Turtle feeding and a children's play corner give Mina A' Salam an edge with families.

☑ Top Tips

▶ If you are staying at a Madinat hotel here or eating at one of the restaurants, your *abra* shuttle is free.

▶ Make dinner or brunch reservations at least one week ahead for any of the restaurants.

▶ Take advantage of happy hour deals offered at many Madinat bars.

▶ Maps are available at several information points.

✗ Take a Break

Enjoy a long cold drink or cocktail at the **Left Bank** (p79), a welcoming bar overlooking the picturesque canals.

Book early for delicious seafood with Madinat and Burj Al Arab views at chic and sophisticated **Pierchic** (p77).

Top Sights
Burj Al Arab

The Burj's graceful silhouette – meant to evoke the sail of a dhow (traditional wooden cargo vessel) – is to Dubai what the Eiffel Tower is to Paris. Completed in 1999, this iconic landmark sits on an artificial island and comes with its own helipad and a fleet of chauffeur-driven Rolls Royce limousines. Beyond the striking lobby, with its gold-leaf opulence and attention-grabbing fountain, lie 202 suites with more trimmings than a Christmas turkey.

⊙ Map p74, B2

☏ 04-301 7777

www.burj-al-arab.com

off Jumeirah Rd, Umm Suqeim

Ⓜ Mall of the Emirates

Skyview Bar, Burj Al Arab

Don't Miss

Cocktails with a View

Despite the stratospheric tab, cocktails (Dh320 minimum spend) or afternoon tea (Dh565) in the Burj's famous **Skyview Bar** (☑04-301 7600; ☺1pm-2am Sat-Thu, from 7pm Fri) is a quintessential Dubai experience for many visitors. The capsule-shaped lounge sticks out from the main building on the 27th floor. Guests must be at least 21 years old and booking (far) ahead is essential. As for the outlandish Liberace-meets–Star Trek interiors, all we can say is...welcome to the Burj!

Burj Beaching

Spread your towel on **Sunset Beach** (Umm Suqeim 3; admission free; Ⓜ First Gulf Bank) to swim with the Burj Al Arab in the background as the sun dips into the Gulf. Sunset is also Dubai's last surfing beach, although waves may soon be blocked because of an expansion to the Jumeirah Beach Hotel marina. For now, facilities are limited to a few changing cubicles and a playground.

Optical Effect

The white metal crosspieces at the top of the Burj Al Arab form what is said to be the largest cross in the Middle East – but it's only visible from the sea. By the time this unexpected feature was discovered, it was too late to redesign the tower – the hotel had already put Dubai on the map and become the icon for the city. Go see the cross on a boat charter and decide for yourself. The scale is amazing.

STEVE BACK / GETTY IMAGES ©

☑ Top Tips

▶ In order to get past the lobby without staying at the Burj, you need to book way ahead for a spot in a bar or restaurant (minimum spend).

▶ For a surreal dining experience, book a table at Al Mahara to nosh on fish and seafood while seated before a giant round aquarium.

▶ The Burj's helipad has hosted several sports stunts, most famously a tennis match between Roger Federer and Andre Agassi in 2005.

✗ Take a Break

If you don't want to shell out mega-dirhams at the Burj, find a table with a view at Madinat Jumeirah – for instance at **Bahri Bar** (p79) – or head to the **360°** (p78), a perennially fashionable resto-bar capping a long curved pier.

Local Life
Gallery Hopping around Al Quoz

The most cutting-edge galleries within Dubai's growing art scene cluster in an industrial area called Al Quoz, south of Sheikh Zayed Road. Its main hub is the warehouse complex known as Alserkal Avenue, but there are other key spaces dotted around the area, especially on 4th and 6th Streets. A new crop of urban cafes fuels the arty vibe.

....

❶ Tom & Serg

Fuel up for your gallery hop with coffee and a bite at this loft-style **cafe** (📞056-474 6812; www.tomandserg.com; 15th St; mains Dh36-89; ⏰8am-4pm Sun-Thu, to 5pm Fri & Sat; 🛜; Ⓜ Noor Bank, First Gulf Bank) with concrete floors, exposed pipes and an open kitchen. The menu teems with feel-good food such as homemade muesli, quinoa-felafel wrap and a Reuben made with Wagyu salt beef.

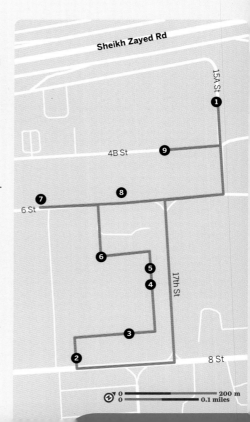

❷ Alserkal Avenue

Edgy contemporary art from the Middle East and beyond has found a home in this sprawling warehouse complex turned **gallery campus** (www.alserkalavenue.ae; near 8th & 17th Sts; M Noor Bank, First Gulf Bank). You'll find some of Dubai's edgiest space here. An adjacent extension is expected to open in 2015.

❸ Gallery Isabelle van den Eynde

This **gallery** (📞 04-323 5052; www.ivde.net; Alserkal Avenue; ⏱ 10am-7pm Sat-Thu; M Noor Bank, First Gulf Bank) has placed some of the most innovative and promising talent from the Middle East, North Africa and South Asia into the spotlight.

❹ The cARTel

Deep in the industrial Al Quoz arts district, this concept fashion **boutique** (📞 04-388 4341; www.thecartel.me; Alserkal Avenue; ⏱ 10am-8pm Sun-Thu, noon-8pm Sat; M Noor Bank, First Gulf Bank) pushes the boundaries when it comes to fashion and accessories. Look for 'wearable art' by an international roster of avant-garde designers.

❺ The Fridge

The Fridge hosts regular **concerts** (📞 04-347 7793; www.thefridgedubai.com; Alserkal Avenue, 8th St near 17th St; M Noor Bank, First Gulf Bank) focusing on local talent still operating below the radar. The line-up defines eclectic and may hopscotch from swing to opera and jazz to pop, sometimes all in one night.

❻ Carbon 12

A minimalist white-cube **space** (📞 04-340 6016; www.carbon12dubai.com; Alserkal Avenue, enter 8th St; ⏱ 11.30am-7pm Sat-Thu; M Noor Bank, First Gulf Bank) presents the gamut of contemporary forms of expression created by established international artists. Some of them have roots in the Middle East, such as Tehran-born New York resident Sara Rahbar.

❼ Third Line

A pioneer in Dubai's gallery scene and one of the city's most exciting venues for contemporary Middle Eastern art, **Third Line** (📞 04-341 1367; www.thethirdline.com; 6th St; ⏱ 10am-7pm Sat-Thu; M Noor Bank, First Gulf Bank) represents around 30 artists, including Emiratis Lamya Gargash and Ebtisam Abdulaziz.

❽ Courtyard

Flanked by an eccentric hodgepodge of buildings that makes it look like a miniature movie-studio set, this **complex** (📞 04-347 5050; www.courtyard-uae.com; 6th St, nr 17th; M Noor Bank, First Gulf Bank) contains design shops, galleries, a community theatre and other creative enterprises.

❾ Lime Tree Cafe

Wrap up your tour at this comfy Euro-style **cafe** (📞 04-325 6325; www.thelimetreecafe.com; 4B St; snacks Dh20-55; ⏱ 8am-6pm; 🛜; M Noor Bank) famous for its carrot cake, sandwiches and pasta dishes.

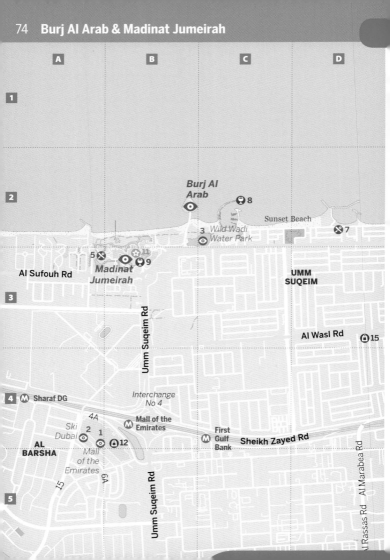

E F G H

THE GULF

For reviews see
- 👁 Top Sights   p68
- 👁 Sights   p76
- ❌ Eating   p77
- 🍷 Drinking   p78
- ⭐ Entertainment   p80
- 🛍 Shopping   p80

0   1 km
0   0.5 miles

Kite Beach   Kite Beach
4

🍷10

📦14

🔒13

6 ❌

Jumeirah Rd

UMM SUQEIM 1

JUMEIRAH

Al Wasl Rd

SAFA

Interchange No 3 (Exit 43)

Ⓜ Noor Bank

Sheikh Zayed Rd

4B St
6

17th St

Al Manara Rd

8

AL QUOZ

Sights

Mall of the Emirates SHOPPING MALL

1 ◎ Map p74, A4

Home to Ski Dubai, a community theatre, an ultraluxe 24-screen multiplex cinema and – let's not forget – 560 stores... and counting (an expansion should be completed in 2015), MoE is one of Dubai's most popular malls. With narrow walkways and no daylight, it can feel a tad claustrophobic at peak times except in the Italian-arcade-style Galeria lidded by a vaulted glass ceiling. (☎04-409 9000; www.malloftheemirates.com; Sheikh Zayed Rd, Interchange No 4, Al Barsha; ◷10am-10pm Sat-Wed, to midnight Thu & Fri; Mall of the Emirates)

Ski Dubai SKIING

2 ◎ Map p74, A4

Skiing in the desert? Where else but in Dubai. The city's most incongruous attraction is a faux winter wonderland built right into the gargantuan Mall of the Emirates. It comes complete with ice sculptures and live penguins, a tiny toboggan run, five ski runs (the longest being 400m) and a Freestyle Zone with jumps and rails.

Novices and kids will enjoy the snow park for its colour-lit igloo and tobogganing hill. The chemical-free snow is generated by snow guns at night. Note that there are separate charges for hats (from Dh55), gloves (Dh20) and lockers (Dh25). (☎04-409 4000; www.skidxb.com; Mall of the Emirates, Al Barsha; Snow Park admission adult/child Dh150/140, 2hr ski pass Dh200/170, penguin encounters from Dh150; ◷10am-11pm Sun-Wed, 10am-midnight Thu, 9am-midnight Fri, 9am-11pm Sat; ; Mall of the Emirates)

Wild Wadi Water Park WATER PARK

3 ◎ Map p74, C2

When the kids grow weary of the beach and hotel pool, you'll score big-time by bringing them to Wild Wadi. Over a dozen ingeniously interconnected rides follow a vague theme about Arabian adventurer Juha and his friend Sinbad the Sailor who get shipwrecked together. There are plenty of gentle rides for tots, plus a big-wave pool and a white-water rapids 'river'. (☎04-348 4444; www.wildwadi.com; Jumeirah Rd; admission over 110cm Dh245/under 110cm 185; ◷10am-6pm Nov-Feb, to 7pm Mar-May & Sep-Oct, to 8pm Jun-Aug; ; Mall of the Emirates)

Kite Beach BEACH

4 ◎ Map p74, F2

Also known as Sheikh Hamdan Beach, this long pristine stretch of white sand is super clean and has lots of activities, including kite surfing, soap football, beach tennis, beach volleyball and kayaking. There are showers, toilets and changing facilities, plus great views of the Burj Al Arab. It gets very busy on weekends (Friday and Saturday). (Sheikh Hamdan Beach; 2D St, Umm Suqeim 1; admission free; Noor Bank)

Ski Dubai

Eating

Pai Thai
THAI $$$

5 Map p74, A3

An *abra* ride, a canalside table and candlelight are the hallmarks of a romantic night out and this enchanting spot sparks on all cylinders. If your date doesn't make you swoon, then the beautifully crafted Thai dishes should still ensure an unforgettable evening. Or come for Friday brunch (with/without alcohol Dh240/190). Book weeks ahead. (☏04-366 6730; www.jumeirah.com; Dar Al Masyaf Hotel, Madinat Jumeirah, Umm Suqeim 3; mains Dh60-195; ⊙6.30-11.30pm; Ⓜ Mall of the Emirates)

Pierchic
SEAFOOD $$$

Looking for a place to drop an engagement ring into a glass of champagne? Make reservations (far in advance) at this impossibly romantic seafood house (see ◎ Madinat Jumeirah, Map p74, B3) capping a long pier with front-row views of the Burj Al Arab and Madinat Jumeirah. The menu is a foodie's daydream, from the champagne ceviche to the poached lobster, all prepared with passion and panache. (☏04-366 6730; www.madinatjumeirah.com; Al Qasr, Madinat Jumeirah, Al Sufouh Rd, Umm Suqeim 3; mains Dh100-240; ⊙noon-3pm & 6.30-11pm; Ⓜ Mall of the Emirates)

Top Tip

Meals on Wheels Hit Dubai

Gourmet food trucks, the export hits from the US and the UK, finally started rolling into Dubai in 2014. Here are some of the pioneers:

SALT (@findsalt) Dubai's first mobile kitchen in a classic silver Airstream serves chicken and Wagyu burgers and has a semi-residency at Kite Beach.

Ghaf Kitchen (@ghafkitchen) Upgraded British comfort food sold from a 1962 Citroen H van found rusting in a field in Normandy, France. Pops up at parties, markets, concerts and other special events.

Jake's Food Truck (@thefoodtruckdubai) Gourmet bagel burgers are the stock in trade of this jazzy painted van.

Turath Al Mandi
YEMENI **$$**

6 Map p74, H2

An aroma of the daily feast wafts from the kitchen of this authentic Arabian restaurant specialising in traditional food from Yemen. A must-try is *mandi* – the national dish – which stars chicken or mutton slow-cooked in a special oven and served over flavoured rice. (☏04-395 3555; www.turath-almandi.ae; Villa 503, Jumeirah Rd, Jumeirah 3; mains Dh42-84; ⊗noon-midnight; 🛜; Ⓜ Noor Bank)

Bu Qtair
FISH **$$**

7 Map p74, D2

Always packed to the gills, this seaside shack is a Dubai institution, famous for serving some of the freshest fish in town, marinated in a fragrant masala (curry) sauce and prepared to order. There's no menu, so just point to what you'd like (Note: the menu includes unsustainable species such as hammour), then lug your cooked-up loot to a rickety plastic table and chow down. (4D St, Umm Suqeim 1; meals Dh40-70; ⊗6.30-11.30pm; Ⓜ Noor Bank)

Al Mahara
SEAFOOD **$$$**

A lift posing as a submarine deposits you at a gold-leaf-clad tunnel spilling into Dubai's most extravagant restaurant (see ⦿ Burj Al Arab, Map p74, B2) whose name translates as 'oyster shell'. Tables orbit a circular floor-to-ceiling aquarium where clownfish flit and baby sharks dart as their sea bass and halibut cousins are being...devoured. Pretty surreal. Dress code and no children under 12 for dinner. (☏04-301 7600; www.jumeirah.com; lower fl, Burj Al Arab; mains Dh320-655; ⊗lunch & dinner; Ⓜ Mall of the Emirates)

Drinking

360°
BAR, CLUB

8 Map p74, C2

Capping a long curved pier, this alfresco playground still hasn't lost its grip on the crowd after many years of music, mingling and magical views of the Burj Al Arab, especially when the sun slips seaward. On weekends (guest list) there are top-notch DJs spinning house for happy hotties; other nights are mellower. (☏04-406 8741; www.jumeirah.com; Jumeirah Beach Hotel, Jumeirah Rd, Umm Suqeim; ⏱5pm-2am Sun-Wed, 5pm-1.30am Thu-Sat; 🛜; Ⓜ Mall of the Emirates)

Bahri Bar
BAR

This chic bar (see ◉ Madinat Jumeirah, Map p74, B3) drips with rich Arabian decor and has a fabulous verandah laid with Persian carpets and big cane sofas where you can take in gorgeous views of the Burj Al Arab. The vibe is very grown-up – the kind of place you take your parents for sunset drinks. (☏04-366 6730; Mina A'Salam Hotel, Madinat Jumeirah; ⏱4pm-2am Sat-Mon, to 3am Tue-Fri; Ⓜ Mall of the Emirates)

Pacha Ibiza Dubai
RESTAURANT, CLUB

 9   Map p74, B3

This legendary nightclub now brings its Balearic sound to a dramatic three-level space at Madinat. Evenings start with dinner and a live show of singers, dancers and acrobats in the main room, which is later heated up by local and international house DJs. Alternative sounds rule the upstairs Red Room while the rooftop is a dedicated *sheesha* and chill zone. (☏04-567 0000; www.pacha.ae; main entrance, Souk Madinat Jumeirah; ⏱8pm-3am Tue-Sat; Ⓜ Mall of the Emirates)

Mazology
MOCKTAILS

10   Map p74, G2

This ubercool beach hangout is popular with local hipsters crouched in lively conversation on white sofas, puffing on a *sheesha* and swilling exotic-looking drinks while being showered by high-octane sounds. Sounds just like your ordinary Dubai nightspot? Not exactly, for there's absolutely no booze in those drinks.

The lounge is part of the Bait Al Bahar, a three-story venue that also includes an Emirati restaurant and a beachfront diner. It's next to Dubai Offshore Sailing Club. (☏04-394 4441; Bait Al Bahar, waterfront; ⏱6am-2am; Ⓜ Noor Bank)

Agency
WINE BAR

Madinat's Agency (see ◉ Madinat Jumeirah, Map p74, B3) is a civilised spot for pre-dinner drinks with a romantic terrace overlooking the Madinat canals. Happy hour runs from 5pm to 8pm Saturday to Thursday. (☏04-366 6730; www.jumeirah.com; Souk Madinat Jumeirah, Umm Suqeim 3; ⏱1pm-1am Sun-Wed, to 2am Thu, 4pm-2am Fri, 5pm-1am Sat; Ⓜ Mall of the Emirates)

Left Bank
BAR

The waterside tables next to the *abra* station are great for tête-à-têtes, but the real party is inside where a backlit bar, giant mirrors, leather club chairs and chill beats create a dynamic lounge scene (see ◉ Madinat Jumeirah, Map p74, B3). Ladies scores three free vodka drinks on Wednesdays between 8pm and 10pm. (📞04-368 6171; Waterfront Promenade, Souk Madinat Jumeirah; ⏰9am-2am Sat-Tue, to 3am Wed-Fri; 📶; Ⓜ Mall of the Emirates)

Entertainment

Dubai Community Theatre & Arts Centre THEATRE

This thriving performance venue (see **12** ⊙ Map p74, B4) at the Mall of the Emirates puts on all sorts of diversions, from classical concerts to Bollywood retrospectives, Arabic folklore to large-scale mural projects. Much support is given to Emirati talent, making this a good place to plug into the local scene. (DUCTAC; 📞04-341 4777; www.ductac.org; top fl, Mall of the Emirates; Ⓜ Mall of the Emirates)

Madinat Theatre THEATRE

11 Map p74, B3

The program at this 442-seat theatre at Souk Madinat is largely calibrated to the cultural cravings of British expats. Expect plenty of crowd-pleasing entertainment ranging from popular West End imports to standup comedy and Russian ballet. (📞04-366 6546; www.madinattheatre.com; Souk Madinat Jumeirah, Umm Suqeim 3; Ⓜ Mall of the Emirates)

Shopping

Mall of the Emirates MALL

12 Map p74, B4

With 560 stores (more after an extension in 2015), MoE is (another)

one of Dubai's megamalls with retail options ranging from high street to haute couture, but with precious few local or regional contenders. Anchor stores include Harvey Nichols and a vast Carrefour supermarket. (📞04-409 9000; www.malloftheemirates.com; Sheikh Zayed Rd, Interchange 4, Al Barsha; ⏰10am-10pm Sat-Wed, to midnight Thu & Fri; Ⓜ Mall of the Emirates)

Aizone FASHION

Lose yourself for hours in this enormous Lebanese fashion emporium (see **12** ⊙ Map p74, B4) with hard-to-find trendy labels and snappy fashions for twirling on the dance floor. Look for the latest threads from Bibelot, Juicy Couture, Spy and Lotus. (📞04-347 9333; Mall of the Emirates; ⏰10am-midnight; Ⓜ Mall of the Emirates)

West LA Boutique FASHION & ACCESSORIES

13 🔒 Map p74, H2

Dubai's hipster crowd circles for the latest garb, cosmetics, jewellery, shoes, bags and other trendy must-haves actually sourced by savvy buyers around the globe, not just in West Los Angeles. The selection is huge, the vibe electric and prices surprisingly reasonable. Sunset Mall itself has plenty of other fashion-forward boutiques, including Socialista and Rivaage. (📞04-394 4248; www.westlaboutique.com; ground fl, Sunset Mall, Jumeirah Rd, Jumeirah 3; ⏰10am-10pm Sat-Thu, 1.30-10pm Fri; Ⓜ Business Bay)

Yasmine
FASHION & ACCESSORIES

This small boutique (see Map p74, B3) specialises in elegantly patterned shawls and *jalabiyas* (traditional kaftans native to the Gulf). The finest are handmade in Kashmir from pashmina (cashmere) or shahtoosh (the down hair of a Tibetan antelope). Machine-made shawls start at Dh150. (📞04-368 6115; www.jalabiatyasmine.com; Souk Madinat Jumeirah, Al Sufouh Rd, Umm Suqeim 3; ⏰10am-11pm; Ⓜ Mall of the Emirates)

Camel Company
SOUVENIRS

If you can slap a camel on it, Camel Company (see Ⓜ Madinat Jumeirah, Map p74, B3) has it. This is hands-down the best spot for camel souvenirs: plush stuffed camels that sing when you squeeze them, camels in Hawaiian shirts, on T-shirts, coffee cups, mouse-pads, notebooks, greeting cards and fridge magnets. (📞04-368 6048; www.camelcompany.ae; Souk Madinat Jumeirah; ⏰10am-11pm; Ⓜ Mall of the Emirates)

Lata's
SOUVENIRS

Ignore the kitsch and look for quality Arabian and Middle Eastern souvenirs (see Ⓜ Madinat Jumeirah, Map p74, B3), such as Moroccan lamps, brass coffee tables, *khanjars* (traditional curved daggers), silver prayer holders and Bedouin jewellery. Browse around or tell the staff what you're after, and they'll steer you right to it. (📞04-368 6216; Souk Madinat Jumeirah; ⏰10am-11pm; Ⓜ Mall of the Emirates)

Garderobe
VINTAGE

14 🔒 Map p74, G2

This is the place to come to snag a one-off vintage item at an affordable price. The preloved designer labels and accessories are in tip-top condition and often include items by Chanel, Hermès, Alexander Wang and Gucci. It's a concept that has proven to be a big hit here, particularly among the expatriate community. (📞04-394 2753; www.garderobe.ae; Jumeirah Rd, Umm Suqeim 1; Ⓜ Noor Bank)

O' de Rose
FASHION & ACCESSORIES

15 🔒 Map p74, D3

It helps if you love bold colours and patterns when shopping at this delightful boutique ensconced in a residential villa and run by a trio of free-spirited cousins from Beirut. Their passion for unusual things is reflected in the selection of postmodern ethnic-chic clothing, accessories, art and home decor created mostly by indie designers from around the region. (📞04-348 7990; www.o-derose.com; 999 Al Wasl Rd, Umm Suqeim 2; ⏰10am-8pm; Ⓜ Noor Bank)

Explore

Downtown Dubai

Downtown Dubai is the city's vibrant urban hub and a key destination for visitors. Its pinnacle is the Burj Khalifa – the world's tallest building – which dwarfs the shop- and attraction-loaded Dubai Mall and Burj Lake where the dancing Dubai Fountain enchants adoring crowds. With lots of hip cafes, restaurants and bars, it's easy to spend an entire day here without ever leaving.

NIKADA / GETTY IMAGES ©

The Sights in a Day

☀ Make your way to the Dubai International Finance Centre, grab a seat in one of the numerous cafes and watch adrenalin-charged bankers in heated conversation. Time for a dose of culture, so head over to **Gate Village** (p90) and check out superb contemporary Middle Eastern art at the sophisticated galleries here before settling down for a protein-filled Japanese lunch at **Zuma** (p93).

☀ Cab or metro it to the **Dubai Mall** (p84) and visit the watery wonderland of the **Aquarium** (p85) before giving your credit cards a workout. Briefly pop across to the Arabian-themed **Souk Al Bahar** (p90) before heading up the **Burj Khalifa** (p86) to pinpoint the sights from above. Wind down the afternoon with alfresco happy hour drinks at **Calabar** (p98) or **Cabana** (p97).

☾ Stake out a terrace table in a restaurant flanking the **Dubai Fountain** (p85) to watch the choreographed dance, music and light shows while tucking into your steak or salad. Post-dinner options include cocktails with views of the glittering skyscrapers at **Neos** (p97), joining locals for *sheesha* (water pipe) at **Nar** (p97) or smooth jazz at the **Blue Bar** (p99).

 Top Sights
Dubai Mall (p84)
Burj Khalifa (p86)

♥ **Best of Dubai**
Eating
Milas (p94)
Zaroob (p93)

Drinking
Neos (p97)
Calabar (p98)
Kris Kros (p97)

For Kids
Dubai Aquarium & Underwater Zoo (p85)
KidZania (p91)

Getting There

Ⓜ **Metro** The Red Line conveniently runs along the entire length of Sheikh Zayed Road. Major stations are Financial Centre, Emirates Towers, Burj Khalifa/Dubai Mall and World Trade Centre.

Top Sights
Dubai Mall

The 'mother of all malls' is much more than the sum of its 1200 stores: it's a veritable family entertainment centre with such crowd magnets as a huge aquarium, an amusement park with thrill rides and arcade games, an Olympic-sized ice rink and a genuine dinosaur skeleton. It also boasts a gorgeous souq, a designer fashion avenue with catwalk and its own glossy monthly magazine. And as if that wasn't enough, the mall underwent further expansion from 2013 through 2015.

◉ Map p88, B5

☎04-362 7500

www.thedubaimall.com

Sheikh Mohammed bin Rashid Blvd

◷10am-midnight

Ⓜ Burj Khalifa/Dubai Mall

Dubai Mall exterior

Don't Miss

Dubai Fountain

This choreographed dancing **fountain** (Burj Lake; admission free; ⊘ shows 1pm & 1.30pm Sat-Thu, 1.30pm & 2pm Fri, every 30min 6-11pm daily; Ⓜ Burj Khalifa/Dubai Mall) is spectacularly set in the middle of a giant lake against the backdrop of the glittering Burj Khalifa. Water undulates as gracefully as a belly dancer, arcs like a dolphin and surges as high as 150m, all synced to stirring soundtracks from classical, Arabic and world music. There are plenty of great vantage points, including from some of the restaurants at Souk Al Bahar, the bridge linking Souk Al Bahar with Dubai Mall, and the Dubai Mall waterfront terrace.

Dubai Aquarium & Underwater Zoo

Dubai Mall's most mesmerising sight is this gargantuan **aquarium** (🖅 04-448 5200; www.thedubai aquarium.com; ground fl, Dubai Mall; tunnel & zoo adult/child 3-12yr Dh70/55; ⊘ 10am-10pm Sun-Wed, to midnight Thu-Sat; Ⓜ Burj Khalifa/Dubai Mall), where thousands of beasties flit and dart amid artificial coral. Sharks and rays are top attractions, but other denizens include sumo-sized groupers and massive schools of pelagic fish. You can view quite a lot for free from the outside or pay to enter the walk-through tunnel. Tickets also include access to the Underwater Zoo upstairs, whose undisputed star is a 5m-long Australian crocodile named King Croc.

Dubai Dino

The Jurassic era meets the future in Dubai Mall's Souk Dome, the new home of *Amphicoelias brontodiplodocus,* an almost complete 155-million-year-old dinosaur skeleton unearthed in Wyoming in 2008. The long-necked lizard stands nearly 8m tall and measures 24m long – including its whiplike tail – thus filling up the better part of the arched and dramatically lit atrium.

☑ Top Tips

▶ Pick up a map and store directory from one of the staffed information desks or consult the interactive electronic store finders.

▶ The Mall is busiest on Thursday and Friday evenings.

▶ For close-ups of the Dubai Fountain show, book a cruise aboard an *abra* (wooden ferry) that sets sail on Burj Lake between 5.45pm and 11.15pm (Dh65).

▶ Wi-fi is free, but for now you need a United Arab Emirates (UAE) mobile-phone number to register.

✘ Take a Break

Ice-cream fans will be in ecstasy over the wonderfully creamy flavours of **Morelli's Gelato** (🖅 04-339 9053; www.morellisgelato.com; lower ground fl; per scoop Dh17; ⊘ 10am-midnight).

If you want to sample the delicious diversity of modern Emirati cuisine, seek out the sleekly designed **Milas** (p94).

Top Sights
Burj Khalifa

The Burj Khalifa is a ground-breaking feat of architecture and engineering with two observation decks on the 124th and 148th floors as well as the At.mosphere restaurant-bar on the 122nd. The world's tallest building pierces the sky at 828m (seven times the height of Big Ben) and opened on 4 January 2010, only six years after excavations began. Up to 13,000 workers toiled day and night, putting up a new floor in as little as three days.

Map p88, B4

www.atthetop.ae

Sheikh Mohammed bin Rashid Blvd, entry lower ground fl, Dubai Mall

8.30am-midnight, last entry 45min before closing

M Burj Khalifa/Dubai Mall

Dubai cityscape with Burj Khalifa

Don't Miss

At the Top Observation Deck

Taking in the views from the world's tallest building is a deservedly crave-worthy experience and a trip to the **At the Top** (adult/child 4-12yr/fast track Dh125/95/300, surcharge 3-7pm Dh25) observation deck on the 124th floor (452m) is the most popular way to do it. High-powered telescopes (extra fee) help bring even distant developments into focus and cleverly simulate the same view at night and 35 years ago. Getting to the deck means passing various multimedia exhibits until a double-decker lift zips you up at 10m per second.

At the Top Sky

To truly be on the world's highest observation platform, head to **At the Top Sky** (Dh500) on the 148th floor (555m). A visit here is set up like a hosted VIP experience with refreshments, a guided tour and an interactive screen where you 'fly' to city landmarks by hovering your hands over high-tech sensors. Afterwards, you're escorted to the 125th floor (456m) to be showered with interesting tidbits about Dubai and the Burj and to see more sights in the interactive A Falcon's Eye View.

At.mosphere

The food may not be out of this world, but the views are certainly stellar from the world's highest **restaurant** (☎04-888 3828; www.atmosphereburjkhalifa. com; mains Dh200-650; ☉12.30-2.30pm & 3pm-2am; ☏) on the 122nd floor (442m). Richly decorated in warm mahogany, limestone and thick carpets, the dining room oozes a sophisticated ambience while the compact menu lets quality meats and seafood shine. There's also a lounge if you just want a drink. Reservations essential.

☑ **Top Tips**

▶ Timed tickets are available at the ticket counter or online up to 30 days in advance. Book early, especially if you want to go up at sunset.

▶ If you can't get a regular ticket, you can still get in by shelling out serious dirham for instant fast-track admission.

▶ On hazy days when views are not great, it's better to visit at night.

▶ Budget at least two hours for your visit.

▶ For a more in-depth experience, you can rent audioguides for Dh25.

✖ **Take a Break**

The Burj has its own **cafe** on the ground floor serving coffee and snacks.

Dubai Mall (p84) has dozens of eateries, from food court classics to upscale dining overlooking the Dubai Fountain.

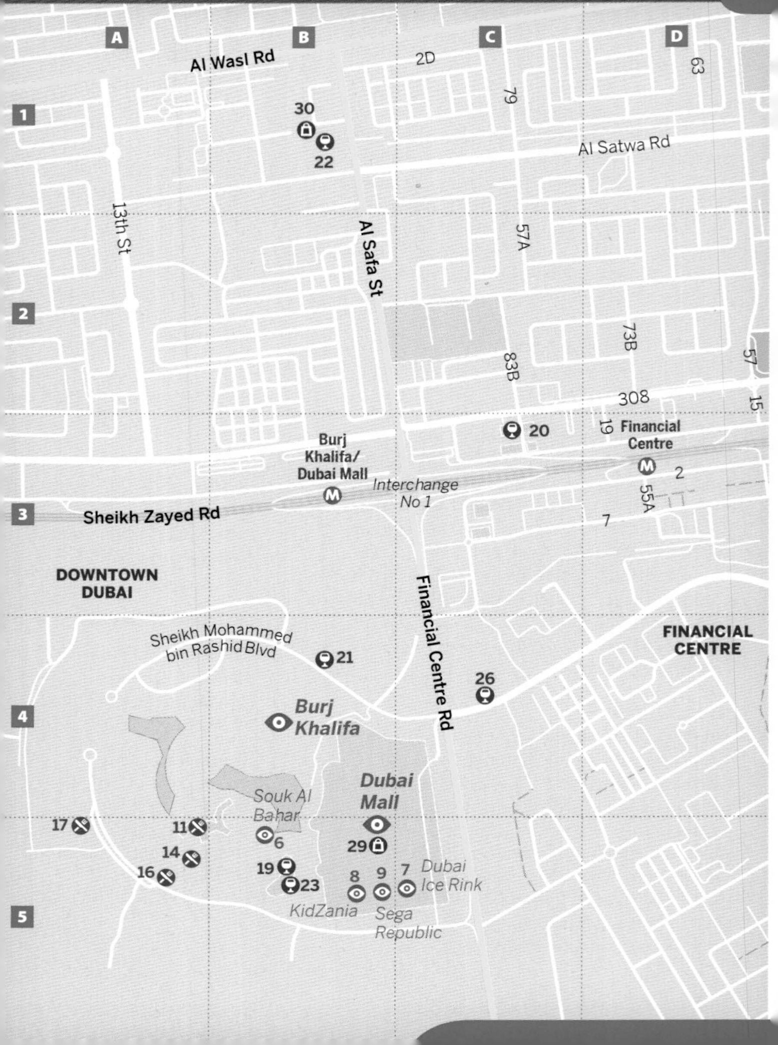

A   B   C   D

Al Wasl Rd

2D

63

1

30

22

Al Satwa Rd

13th St

Al Safa St

79

57A

57

2

83B

73B

308

57

19

15

Q 20

Financial
Centre

2

M

55A

3 Sheikh Zayed Rd

Burj
Khalifa/
Dubai Mall
M Interchange
No 1

7

**DOWNTOWN
DUBAI**

Sheikh Mohammed
bin Rashid Blvd

**FINANCIAL
CENTRE**

21

26

4

*Burj
Khalifa*

Financial Centre Rd

*Dubai
Mall*

17

11

*Souk Al
Bahar*

6

29

14

16

19

23

KidZania

8 9 7 *Dubai
Ice Rink*

*Sega
Republic*

5

E 49

F

G Satwa Roundabout

H

1

Al Satwa Rd
6B   8A
10B
21   19   17   13A   SATWA   57A   6C   33A   22

20B   20A
22B   22B
30A

308   5   ❷27   22B   24   ❷   Al Dhiyafah St   39B   24A   31B   24

11   Za'abeel Roundabout   54   36   ❸32 🔒

Emirates Towers   Ⓜ   Sheikh Zayed Rd   Ⓜ   World Trade Centre   Za'abeel Park   Za'abeel

18 13
25 ✖✖   12
10 ✖   Ayyam Gallery   Opera Gallery   17   ❷28   2nd Za'abeel Rd   ZA'ABEEL
31 🔒   5
4   Gate Village   312
Empty Quarter   3   1 ✖15
Cuadro

Horse Racecourse

For reviews see
👁 Top Sights   p84
◉ Sights   p90
✖ Eating   p92
🍷 Drinking   p97
⭐ Entertainment   p99
🛍 Shopping   p99

0 _____ 500 m
0 _____ 0.25 miles

Sights

Gate Village
GALLERIES

1 Map p88, E3

Two wooden bridges link the massive Dubai International Finance Centre (DIFC) to Gate Village, a modernist cluster of 10 midrise stone-clad towers built around walkways and small piazzas. This is where many of Dubai's high-end Middle Eastern art galleries, including Ayyam and Cuadro, have set up shop alongside a couple of posh eateries such as Zuma. (DIFC, Sheikh Zayed Rd; M Emirates Towers)

Ayyam Gallery
GALLERY

2 Map p88, E3

With branches at Gate Village and in Al Quoz as well as in Beirut and London, this top gallery's main mission is to promote emerging Middle Eastern artists and to introduce their often provocative, political and feminist work and voices to a wider audience outside the region itself. (☑04-439 2395; www.ayyamgallery.com; Bldg 3, Gate Village, DIFC; ⏱10am-10pm Sun-Wed, 2-10pm Thu & Sat; M Emirates Towers)

Cuadro
GALLERY

3 Map p88, E3

In a fabulous space taking up the entire ground floor of Gate Village's Building 10, this highly regarded gallery shines the spotlight on contemporary artists and sculptors from both the West and Middle East and also presents lectures, workshops and panel discussions. (☑04-425 0400; www.cuadro art.com; Bldg 10, Gate Village; ⏱noon-6pm Sat, 10am-8pm Sun-Thu; M Emirates Towers)

Empty Quarter
GALLERY

4 Map p88, E3

It's always worth stopping by this top-notch gallery focused entirely on fine-art photography created by accomplished shutterbugs from around the globe. Shows often capture the zeitgeist with evocative, provocative or political themes such as Miguel Angel Sanchez' recent exhibition, 'The Faces of Gaza'. (☑04-323 1210; www.theempty quarter.com; Bldg 2, Gate Village, DIFC; ⏱10am-8pm Sun-Thu; M Emirates Towers)

Opera Gallery
GALLERY

5 Map p88, E3

More an art showroom than a classically curated gallery, Opera caters to collectors of artistic heavyweights in genres as varied as pop art, calligraphy and landscapes. One section of the beautiful bilevel space is reserved for contemporary artists from the Middle East. (☑04-323 0909; www.opera gallery.com; Bldg 3, Gate Village; ⏱10am-8pm Sun-Thu; M Emirates Towers)

Souk Al Bahar
MALL

6 Map p88, B5

Designed in contemporary Arabian style, this attractive mall is Downtown Dubai's answer to Madinat Jumeirah. Meaning 'Market of the Sailor', it features natural-stone walkways, high

CHRIS MELLOR / GETTY IMAGES ©

Souk Al Bahar is linked to Dubai Mall by a bridge over Burj Lake

arches and front-row seats overlooking Dubai Fountain from several of its restaurants and bars, including Baker & Spice, Left Bank and Karma Kafe. It's located next to Dubai Mall. (📞04-362 7012; www.soukalbahar.ae; Downtown Dubai; ⊙10am-10pm Sat-Thu, 2-10pm Fri; Ⓜ Burj Khalifa/Dubai Mall)

Dubai Ice Rink   ICE SKATING

7 ◎ Map p88, C5

This Olympic-sized ice rink is ringed with cafes and restaurants and can even be converted into a concert arena. Sign up for a private or group class if you're a little wobbly in the knees. There are also night-time disco sessions for moving and shaking it up on the ice. (📞04-437 1111; www.dubai icerink.com; ground fl, Dubai Mall; per session incl skates Dh60-80; ⊙10am-midnight; Ⓜ Burj Khalifa/Dubai Mall)

KidZania   AMUSEMENT PARK

8 ◎ Map p88, B5

For guilt-free shopping without your kids, drop them off in this edutaining miniature city – complete with a school, a fire station, a hospital and a bank – where they get to dress up and slip into adult roles to playfully explore what it's like to be a firefighter, doctor, mechanic, pilot or other professional.

They even earn a salary with which they can buy goods and services, thus learning the value of money. Kids must be at least 120cm tall to be dropped off. There's also a special toddler zone and a baby care centre. (📞04-448 5222; www.kidzania.ae; 2nd fl, Dubai Mall; adult/child 4-16yr Dh95/140, child 2-3yr Dh95; ⏰9am-9pm Sun-Wed, 9am-11pm Thu, 10am-11pm Fri & Sat; Ⓜ Burj Khalifa/Dubai Mall)

Sega Republic AMUSEMENT PARK

 9 ⊙ Map p88, B5

Bing, boing, beep, zap – this bilevel indoor amusement park with 170 arcade games and 15 tame to (mildly) terrifying thrill rides is a visual and sensory onslaught. Among the adrenaline boosters: race simulators, a small roller

Local Life
Farmers Markets

With the local-seasonal-organic trend finally engulfing Dubai, it's no surprise that farmers markets are increasingly making inroads. Aside from the traditional daily fruit and vegetable market adjacent to the Fish Market in Deira, there's now the hip weekly **Ripe Food & Craft Market** (Map p88, H3; 📞04-380 7602; Gate 1, Za'abeel Park; ⏰9am-2pm Fri Nov-Mar; Ⓜ Al Jafiliya) in beautiful Za'abeel Park. It features not only fruit and veg but also local honey, nuts, spices and eggs, plus arts and crafts, food stations and locally roasted gourmet coffee. Pretty much all you need for a picnic under the palms. During the same months you'll also find a small courtyard market in Souk Madinat Jumeirah.

coaster, a free-fall tower and a mechanical tornado. Some rides have height restrictions. Pay per ride or choose from various day passes for unlimited trips. (📞04-448 8484; www.segarepublic.com; 2nd fl, Dubai Mall; attractions Dh15-30, day pass from Dh175; ⏰10am-11pm Sun-Wed, 10am-1am Thu-Sat; Ⓜ Burj Khalifa/Dubai Mall)

Eating

Clé Dubai MIDDLE EASTERN $$$

 10 ✕ Map p88, E3

Australian-born Michelin chef Greg Malouf has decamped to Dubai to open this sensuously styled haven for dedicated foodies and power diners. In his signature approach, he deconstructs the flavour-intense mystique of traditional Middle Eastern dishes and reassembles it into thoroughly contemporary culinary symphonies such as goat *tajine* (stew cooked in a clay pot), salmon kibbeh or hazelnut felafel. (📞04-352 5150; http://cle-dubai. com; Al Fattan Currency House, DIFC; sharing dishes Dh30-285, 2-/3-course lunch Dh95/130; ⏰noon-2am; 🛜; Ⓜ Financial Centre)

Asado ARGENTINE $$$

 11 ✕ Map p88, A5

Meat lovers will be in heaven at this rustic-elegant lair with stellar views of the Burj Khalifa from the terrace tables. Start with a selection of deliciously filled *empanadas*, the traditional Argentine fried dumplings, before treating yourself to a juicy grilled steak or the signature baby goat, slowly tickled to succulent perfection by a charcoal fire. Reservations essential. (📞04-888 3444; www.theaddress.com; Palace Downtown Dubai, Sheikh Mohammed bin Rashid Blvd; mains Dh130-290; 🕑7-11.30pm; Ⓜ Burj Khalifa/Dubai Mall)

Ivy INTERNATIONAL $$$

12 Map p88, E3

Dark oak floors and stained glass set a retro-chic scene at the Dubai edition of this London institution. Aside from a few classic British dishes (such as the signature shepherd's pie), the menu has a distinctly international brasserie bent with everything from gazpacho to foie gras and Sri Lankan lamb curry making appearances. Reservations essential. (📞04-319 8767; www.theivy.ae; ground fl, The Boulevard, Jumeirah Emirates Towers; mains Dh120-360, 2-/3-hour business lunch Dh120/150, brunch Dh300-600; 🕑noon-11pm Sat-Wed, to 11.30pm Thu & Fri; 🛜; Ⓜ Emirates Towers)

Zaroob LEBANESE $

13 Map p88, E3

With its open kitchens, baskets billowing with fruit, colourful lanterns and steel shutters festooned with funky graffiti, Zaroob radiates the earthy integrity of a Beirut alley filled with street food stalls. Feast on such delicious but no-fuss food as felafel, shwarma, flat or wrapped *manoush* (Lebanese pizza) sandwiches, *alayet* (tomato stew) or tabbouleh, all typical of the Levant region. (📞04-327 6060; www.zaroob.com;

ground fl, Jumeirah Emirates Towers; dishes Dh8-26; 🕑24hr; 🛜; Ⓜ Emirates Towers)

Baker & Spice INTERNATIONAL $$

The colourful salad bar is the undisputed star at this charming, country-style cafe (see 6 🔘 Map p88, B5). Presented in mouthwatering fashion, it's a seasonal bounty of intriguingly paired organic ingredients (eg lentils perked up with pumpkin cubes and pomegranate seeds). The mains are more conventional but just as tasty. Also a good spot for breakfast. (📞04-425 2240; www.bakerandspiceme.com; Souk Al Bahar; mains Dh45-145; 🕑8am-11pm; 🛜; Ⓜ Burj Khalifa/Dubai Mall)

Thiptara THAI $$$

14 Map p88, A5

Thiptara means 'magic at the water' – very appropriate given its romantic setting in a lakeside pagoda with un-impeded views of the Dubai Fountain. The food is just as impressive, with elegant interpretations of classic Thai dishes perked up by herbs grown by the chef himself. (📞04-428 7888; www.theaddress.com; Palace Downtown Dubai, Sheikh Mohammed bin Rashid Blvd; mains Dh110-200, set menus from Dh299; 🕑dinner; Ⓜ Burj Khalifa/Dubai Mall)

Zuma JAPANESE $$$

15 Map p88, E3

Every dish speaks of refinement in this perennially popular bilevel restaurant that gives classic Japanese fare an up-to-the-minute workout.

No matter if you go for the top-cut sushi morsels (the dynamite spider roll is a serious eye-catcher!), meat and seafood tickled by the robata grill, or such signature dishes as miso-marinated cod, you'll be keeping your taste buds happy. (📞04-425 5660; www.zumarestaurant.com; Gate Village 06, DIFC; set lunches Dh130, mains Dh75-160; ⏰lunch daily, dinner Sat-Wed, to 2am Thu & Fri; 🛜; Ⓜ️Emirates Towers)

Mayrig Dubai
ARMENIAN $$

16 🍴 Map p88, A5

Mayrig's Armenian menu may borrow heavily from Lebanese cuisine, but not without setting its own distinctive flavour accents. Menu stars include *sou beureg* (a flaky cheese-filled pastry), the mouthwatering *fishnah kebab* topped with wild sour cherry sauce, and the lemon zest chocolate cake. There's no alcohol but you can enjoy *sheesha* on the terrace. It's opposite the Al Manzil Hotel. (📞04-279 0300; www.mayrigdubai.com; Sheikh Mohammed bin Rashid Blvd; mains Dh57-85; ⏰noon-12.30am; 🛜; Ⓜ️Burj Khalifa/Dubai Mall)

Leila
LEBANESE $$

17 🍴 Map p88, A5

This Beirut import serves grannie-style rural Lebanese cafe cuisine adapted for the 21st century, ie light, healthy and fresh. The homey decor more than dabbles in the vintage department with its patterned wallpaper, crisp table cloths and floral dishes. Don't miss the spicy potato cubes and the *jebneh mtab-baleh* (white cheese with tomato and oregano). (📞04-448 3384; Sheikh Mohammed bin Rashid Blvd; mains Dh28-78; ⏰9.30am-11pm Sat-Wed, to midnight Thu & Fri; Ⓜ️Burj Khalifa/Dubai Mall)

Milas
EMIRATI $$

Milas (see 29 Ⓐ Map p88, B5) is how Emiratis pronounce *majlis* – the traditional guest reception room. This particular *majlis* has a contemporary look (wood, glass, neon) that goes well with updated riffs on such traditional local dishes as *harees* (sugar-sprinkled cooked wheat) and *makbus* (beef stew). Thoughtful perks: wet handcloths, the complimentary *danqaw* (chickpea) appetizer and a postmeal perfume tray. (📞04-388 2313; http://milas.cc; ground fl, Dubai Mall, Denim Village; mains Dh57-95; ⏰9.30am-11.30pm Sun-Wed, to 12.30am Thu-Sat; Ⓜ️Burj Khalifa/Dubai Mall)

Karma Kafé
ASIAN $$$

At this hip outpost (see 6 Ⓞ Map p88, B5) a large Buddha oversees the dining room dressed in sensuous crimson and accented with funky design details. Though Japan-centric, the menu actually hopscotches around Asia with special nods going to the teriyaki tenderloin, the lava prawns and the Thai calamari. The terrace has grand Dubai Fountain views. Reservations essential. (📞04-423 0909; www.karma-kafe.com; Souk Al Bahar; mains Dh75-150; ⏰3pm-2am Sun-Thu, noon-2am Fri & Sat; Ⓜ️Burj Khalifa/Dubai Mall)

Dubai Fountain (p85) at night

Rivington Grill BRITISH $$$

This London transplant (see 6 Map
p88, B5) serves classic British food in a
couldn't-be-more-Dubai location with
a candlelit terrace overlooking the
Dubai Fountain. Not only homesick
Brits give a keen thumbs up to the
fish and chips with poshed-up mushy
peas, beef Wellington with all the
trimmings and the smoked had-
dock fishcakes. (✆04-423 0903; www.
rivingtongrill.ae; Level 3, Souk Al Bahar; mains
Dh95-260; Ⓜ Burj Khalifa/Dubai Mall)

Noodle House ASIAN $$

18 Ⓧ Map p88, E3

The concept at this reliably good
multibranch pan-Asian joint is

simple: sit down at long wooden
communal tables and order by ticking
dishes on a tear-off menu pad. There's
great variety – roast duck to noodle
soups and pad thai – and a spice-level
indicator to please disparate tastes.
Some dishes come in two sizes to
match tummy grumbles. (✆04-319
8088; lower level, Boulevard at Jumeirah
Emirates Towers; mains Dh40-90; Ⓥnoon-
midnight; 🤶🐾; Ⓜ Emirates Towers)

Elevation Burger AMERICAN $

This Virginia-based chain (see 29 Ⓐ
Map p88, B5) proves that there is such a
thing as guilt-free fast food by serving
burgers made entirely from organic,
grass-fed and free-range beef. There
are a dozen toppings to choose from,

Understand

Religion on a Plate

Muslims don't eat pork: it is haram, forbidden by Islam, as pigs are considered unclean. Alcohol is forbidden because it makes followers forgetful of God and prayer. The other major dietary restriction applies to meat: it must be halal, meaning religiously suitable or permitted. The animal must be drained of its blood at the time of slaughter by having its throat cut. That is why much of the red meat slaughtered and sold locally is very pale in colour. In restaurants, you will easily find nonhalal beef – just don't expect your tenderloin to be wrapped in a fatty strip of bacon before it's grilled.

Restaurants & Supermarkets

Some supermarkets sell beef and turkey bacon as an alternative to pork bacon, though hypermarkets such as Carrefour and Spinney's have dedicated 'pork rooms' that sell the real thing – they may not officially be entered by Muslims. To serve pork in a restaurant, you must have a pork licence. Likewise with alcohol, which is generally only served in hotels. If an item on a restaurant menu has been prepared with either alcohol or pork, it must be clearly marked.

Ramadan

The holy month of Ramadan is a time of spiritual contemplation for Muslims, who must fast from sunrise to sunset. Non-Muslim visitors are not expected to fast, but they should not smoke, drink or eat (including gum-chewing) in public during daylight hours. Business premises and hotels make provisions for the nonfasting by erecting screens around dining areas.

Ramadan would seem to be the ideal time to lose weight, yet lots of people pile on the pounds. The fast is broken each day with a communal breakfast comprising something light (such as dates and *laban* – an unsweetened yoghurt drink) before prayers. Then comes *iftar* at which enough food is usually consumed to compensate for the previous hours of abstinence with socialising that continues well into the early hours. With hundreds of restaurants putting on good-value *iftar* buffets, the temptation to overindulge is everywhere.

including caramelised onions and smoky 'elevation' sauce. Carbophobes can trade the bun for lettuce. It's above the ice rink. (☎04-330 8468; www.elevationburger.com; ground fl, Dubai Mall; burgers Dh25-42; ⏰10am-midnight Sun-Wed, to 1am Thu-Sat; Ⓜ Burj Khalifa/Dubai Mall)

Drinking

Neos   BAR

19 Ⓠ Map p88, B5

At this glamour vixen, you can swirl your cosmo with the posh set 63 floors above Dubai Fountain. It takes two lifts to get to this urban den of shiny metal, carpeted floors, killer views and a DJ playing house. (☎04-888 3444; www.theaddress.com; Address Downtown Dubai Hotel; ⏰6pm-2.30am; 🛜; Ⓜ Burj Khalifa/Dubai Mall)

Cabana   BAR, LOUNGE

A laid-back poolside vibe combines with urban sophistication and stellar views of the Burj Khalifa at this alfresco restaurant and terrace lounge (see 29 Ⓔ Map p88, B5). A DJ plays smooth tunes that don't hamper animated conversation. Finish a Dubai Mall shopping spree during happy hour, which runs from 4pm to 8pm. On Tuesdays, women can drink at half price. (☎04-888 3444; www.theaddress. com; 3rd fl, Address Dubai Mall Hotel; ⏰9am-midnight Sun-Thu, to 12.30am Fri & Sat; 🛜; Ⓜ Burj Khalifa/Dubai Mall)

Act   CABARET, CLUB

20 Ⓠ Map p88, C3

To create his Dubai edition of the Box, his burlesque dinner theatre in Vegas, London and New York, entertainment impresario Simon Hammerstein had to think, well...outside the box. So no strippers and raunchy performances here but still a mighty good time featuring artistic and often sexy variety acts to go with your plate of ceviche or *anticuchos de lomo* (beef skewers). (☎04-355 1116; www.theactdubai. com; Shangri-La Hotel, Sheikh Zayed Rd; ⏰8.30pm-3am Sun & Thu, to 1am Mon-Wed; Ⓜ Financial Centre)

Kris Kros   SHEESHA, MOCKTAILS

21 Ⓠ Map p88, B4

Tucked into an office tower with a side view of the Burj Khalifa, funkily furnished Kris Kros does its name justice, as its menu criss-crosses the globe (buffalo wings, burritos, pizza, shwarma etc). What makes the place special, though, is the extensive selection of mocktails and *sheesha,* including such unusual flavours as mango vanilla and bubble gum. (☎04-453 9994; Sheikh Mohammed bin Rashid Blvd; sheesha Dh47, mocktails Dh20-25; 🛜; Ⓜ Burj Khalifa/Dubai Mall)

Nar   SHEESHA

22 Ⓠ Map p88, B1

With a prime position facing City Walk's shallow pond, Nar is a popular cool-kid hangout in the cooler months.

Aside from a large *sheesha* selection, it makes some mean mocktails and has a full menu featuring mezze (appetizers), *mishtah* (topped flatbread), *saroukh* (stuffed bread pockets) and other Lebanese munchables. (☑04-344 3749; City Walk, Al Safa & Al Wasl Rds; sheesha Dh48-75; ⊘9am-1.30am; Ⓜ Burj Khalifa/Dubai Mall)

Calabar
BAR

23 ⊘ Map p88, B5

You'll have plenty of time to study the space-age Burj Khalifa, the eye-candy crowd and the sexy cocktail bar setting while you're waiting...and waiting...for a pricey but potent cocktail at this Latino-themed bar. It's a popular postwork and postmall crawl pit stop with a handy daily happy hour from 6pm to 8pm. (☑04-888 3444; www.theaddress.com; ground fl, Address Downtown Dubai Hotel; ⊘6pm-2.30am; ⎘; Ⓜ Burj Khalifa/Dubai Mall)

40 Kong
BAR

24 ⊘ Map p88, H2

Finance moguls and corporate execs mix it up with cubicle hotties at this intimate rooftop cocktail bar perched atop the 40th floor of the H Hotel with views of the World Trade Centre and Sheikh Zayed Road. The twinkling lanterns and palm trees set romantic accents for postwork or -shopping sundowners, paired with Asian bar bites. (☑04-355 8896; www.40kong.com; 40th fl, H Hotel, Sheikh Zayed Rd; ⊘6pm-3am; ⎘; Ⓜ World Trade Centre)

Harry Ghatto's
KARAOKE BAR

25 ⊘ Map p88, E3

Karaoke kicks off at 10pm, just when happy hour ends oh-so-conveniently in case you need to knock back a couple of drinks to loosen your nerves before belting out your best Beyoncé or 'Bohemian Rhapsody'. There are 1000 songs to choose from, Japanese munchies on the menu and a lively mix of people to (hopefully) cheer you on. (☑04-319 8088; Jumeirah Emirates Towers Hotel, Sheikh Zayed Rd; ⊘noon-3am Sat-Thu, 4pm-3am Fri; ⎘; Ⓜ Emirates Towers)

Double Decker
PUB

26 ⊘ Map p88, C4

You'll feel quite Piccadilly at this boozy, boisterous bilevel pub that's decked out in a London transport theme. Drinks promotions, quiz nights, English Premier League football and better-than-average (by far) pub grub attract a boisterous expat crowd. (☑04-321 1111; Al Murooj Rotana Hotel, cnr Financial Centre Rd & 312th Rd; ⊘noon-3am; ⎘; Ⓜ Financial Centre)

Cavalli Club
CLUB

27 ⊘ Map p88, G2

Black limos jostle for position outside Italian designer Roberto Cavalli's over-the-top lair where beaus and socialites keep the champagne flowing amid a virtual Aladdin's cave of black quartz and Swarovski crystals. Girls, wear those vertiginous heels or risk feeling

Arabian Court at Dubai Mall

frumpy. Boys, dress snappy or forget about it. The entrance is behind the hotel. (📞050-991 0400; http://dubai.cavalli club.com; Fairmont Hotel, Sheikh Zayed Rd; ⏰9.30pm-3am; 🛜; Ⓜ World Trade Centre)

Entertainment

Blue Bar
BAR, LIVE MUSIC

28 ⭐ Map p88, G3

Cool cats of all ages gather in this relaxed joint for some of the finest live jazz and blues in town along with reasonably priced cocktails named after jazz greats (try the Louis Armstrong–inspired Wonderful World). The mostly local talent starts performing at 10pm (Wednesday to Friday only).

(📞04-332 0000; Hotel Novotel World Trade Centre Dubai, 2nd Za'abeel Rd; ⏰2pm-2am; 🛜; Ⓜ World Trade Centre)

Shopping

Dubai Mall
MALL

29 🅐 Map p88, B5

With around 1200 stores, this is not merely the world's largest shopping mall – it's a small city unto itself, with a giant ice rink and aquarium, a dino skeleton, indoor theme parks and 150 food outlets. (📞04-362 7500; www.the dubaimall.com; Sheikh Mohammed bin Rashid Blvd, Downtown Dubai; ⏰10am-midnight; 🛜; Ⓜ Burj Khalifa/Dubai Mall)

Kinokuniya   BOOKS

This bookstore-in-the-round (see 29 Ⓖ Map p88, B5), founded in 1927 Japan, is El Dorado for bookworms. Shelves are stocked with a mind-boggling half a million tomes plus 1000 or so magazines in English, Arabic, Japanese, French, German and Chinese. (☎04-434 0111; www.kinokuniya.com/ae; 2nd fl, Dubai Mall; ⏰10am-midnight; Ⓜ Burj Khalifa/Dubai Mall)

Candylicious   FOOD

Stand under the lollipop tree, watch the candymakers at work or gorge yourself on gourmet popcorn at this colourful candy emporium (see 29 Ⓖ Map p88, B5) stocked to the rafters with everything from jelly beans to halal sweets and gourmet chocolate. Sweet

✅ Top Tip
Dubai Trolley

Getting around Downtown Dubai has never been easy, which is why we're happy to see the arrival of the Dubai Trolley. Its first section, which covers 1km with three stops at the Dubai Mall, the Address Downtown and the Vida Downtown Dubai hotels, should have rolled out by the time you're reading this. When completed, the nostalgic double-decker streetcars, which are powered by electricity, will run for 7km along Mohammed bin Rashid Blvd, linking the mall with the Burj Khalifa, other hotels and the Dubai metro station.

bliss. Just don't tell your dentist. You'll find it next to Dubai Aquarium. (☎04-330 8700; www.candyliciousshop.com; ground fl, Dubai Mall; ⏰10am-midnight; Ⓜ Burj Khalifa/Dubai Mall)

Tehran Persian Carpets & Antiques   GIFTS

The name is misleading, because although it does sell carpets and a handful of antiques, the inventory here (see 6 Ⓞ Map p88, B5) is especially strong when it comes to Iranian decorative items including delicately carved boxes made from gorgeous peacock-coloured turquoise or turquoise-blue decorative plates, fancy stained-glass lamps and plenty of colourful silver jewellery and trinkets. (☎04-420 0515; 1st fl, Souk Al Bahar; Ⓜ Burj Khalifa/Dubai Mall)

Nayomi   LINGERIE

One of Dubai's sexiest stores (see 29 Ⓖ Map p88, B5) stocks push-up bras, high-heeled feathery slippers, slinky night gowns and other nocturnal niceties made in – of all places – Saudi Arabia. In fact, Nayomi, which means 'soft' and 'delicate' in Arabic, is a major brand all over the Middle East with 10 branches around Dubai alone. (☎04-339 8820; www.nayomi.com.sa; 1st fl, Dubai Mall; ⏰10am-midnight; Ⓜ Burj Khalifa/Dubai Mall)

City Walk   MALL

30 Ⓐ Map p88, B1

With only Phase 1 of this low-rise, Euro-style open-air mall completed, there's not much to draw you here in terms of shopping, although the cafes wrapped around a pool – some with a view of the Burj Khalifa – make for an inviting pit stop. Meanwhile, the much larger Phase 2 expansion is taking shape next door. It's located between Al Wasl and Al Satwa Rds. (Al Safa Rd; Ⓜ Burj Khalifa/Dubai Mall)

Bookshop at DIFC   BOOKS
31 🔒 Map p88, E3

This bookshop, cafe, workspace and overall convivial hangout has a hand-picked selection of new and used books about the Middle East and North Africa and also does killer coffee, cookies and croissants. (☏ 050-874 9671; www.bookshop dubai.me; main lobby, Precinct 2 Bldg, DIFC; ⏰ 8am-6pm Sun-Thu; Ⓜ Emirates Towers)

Daiso   GENERAL STORE
Millionaires to wallet-watchers shop at Daiso (see 29 Map p88, B5), Japan's equivalent of the '99 cents' or 'One

Euro' store and nirvana for fans of fun, kitsch and cute trinkets – almost all developed in Japan by Daiso itself. The huge inventory (up to 90,000 items) also includes plenty of practical stuff such as pens, paper towels and packing material. (☏ 04-388 2902; www. daisome.com; lower ground fl, Dubai Mall; ⏰ 10am-midnight; Ⓜ Burj Khalifa/Dubai Mall)

Dubai Flea Market   FLEA MARKET
32 🔒 Map p88, H2

Flea markets are like urban archaeology: you'll need plenty of patience and luck when sifting through other people's trash and detritus, but oh, the thrill when finally unearthing a piece of treasure! Trade malls for stalls and look for bargains amid the piles of preloved stuff that's spilled out of local closets. (www.dubai-flea market.com; Gates 1, 2 & 3 Za'abeel Park; admission Dh5; ⏰ 8am-3pm every 1st Sat Oct-May; Ⓜ Al Jafiliya)

Explore

Dubai Marina & Palm Jumeirah

Dubai Marina is a coveted residential area and its pedestrian-friendly layout also holds plenty of visitor appeal. Stroll past the marina's fancy yachts and futuristic high-rises or head on over to the beach, cafes and shops at the Walk at JBR and the Beach at JBR. Jutting into the Gulf is the Palm Jumeirah, a palm-shaped artificial island loaded with **luxury resorts and residences**.

Explore 103

CHRIS MELLOR / GETTY IMAGES ©

The Sights in a Day

☀ The perfect place to spend a morning in the marina is on the beach. Grab breakfast, coffee or juice at one of the cafes along the **Walk at JBR** (p108), then find your favourite spot to spread your towel on **JBR Open Beach** (p108). For lunch, let your tummy tell you whether to fuel up on salad, sushi or burgers at the **Beach at JBR** (p108) restaurant.

☀ It's pretty hot by now, so hop on the monorail and head to Atlantis The Palm to marvel at groupers and jelly fish at the **Lost Chambers** (p108), before getting wet again at the **Aquaventure Waterpark** (p109). Cab it down to One&Only The Palm for an aperitivo and million-dollar views at the sleek **101 Lounge & Bar** (p115), then catch its boat shuttle back to the mainland.

☾ Wander past yachts and high-rises on the Marina Walk (p104) to dinner with a view, for instance at **Asia Asia** (p112) or **Aquara** (p112). Afterwards, wind down the night with cocktails and more fabulous views at the chic rooftop **Siddharta** (p117) lounge.

For a local's day in Dubai Marina, see p104.

 Local Life

The Marina Walk (p104)

 Best of Dubai

Eating
Fümé (p111)
Indego by Vineet (p111)

Drinking
Jetty Lounge (p116)
Barasti (p116)
Atelier M (p116)
Siddharta (p117)

Dance Clubs
Dek on 8 (p117)
Zero Gravity (p109)
N'Dulge (p119)
Nasimi Beach (p118)

Getting There

Ⓜ **Metro** The Red Line stops at Damac for the Dubai Marina. For the Walk at JBR, the Jumeirah Lakes Towers station is a bit more convenient.

🚊 **Tram** Dubai Tram links Dubai Media City, JBR and Dubai Marina on an 11km loop.

Local Life
The Marina Walk

A saunter along the Marina Walk promenade is delightful, especially after dusk when you can gaze out at the glittering towers and yachts, stop by the dancing fountains and stake out your favourite dinner, drink or *sheesha* (water pipe) spot. Carved from the desert, this is one of the world's largest man-made marinas, centred on a 3km-long canal flanked by a thicket of futuristic high-rises, including the eye-catching twisting Cayan Tower.

❶ Bicycle Cruising

The first rent-a-bike service in the Middle East, **Byky** (www.bykystations.com; 1/2/24 hours Dh20/25/80; ⏲24hr) lets you pick up and drop off bicycles at numerous stations dotted around the Dubai Marina and Palm Jumeirah, including this one next to Spinney's supermarket. All you need to do is register first via its website, which also has full details about how the scheme works. One person can rent

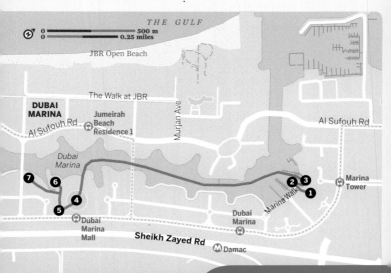

up to four bikes for a minimum of 15 minutes and a maximum of 24 hours.

❷ Sheesha Chilling

This is the prettiest **Reem Al Bawadi** (☎04-452 2525; www.reemalbawadi.com; Marina Walk; sheesha Dh40; ⊙9am-3am; Ⓜ Damac) branch, a local minichain serving regional faves in a dimly lit, endearingly over-the-top *Arabian Nights* setting complete with costumed waiters. The spacious terrace is ideal for kicking back with a *sheesha* while keeping tabs on the marina action.

❸ Water Bus

Marina residents use it to commute, but for visitors a ride on the **Water Bus** (Dubai Marina; tickets Dh3-5, 1-day pass Dh25; ⊙10am-10pm Sat-Wed, to midnight Thu, noon-midnight Fri) offers an inexpensive scenic spin. Boats shuttle between the Marina Walk, Marina Terrace, Marina Mall and the Promenade every 15 minutes. It's especially lovely at sunset or after dark when you float past the show-stopping parade of shimmering towers.

❹ Dubai Marina Mall

With only 160 stores, **Dubai Marina Mall** (☎04-436 1020; www.dubaimarinamall. com; Dubai Marina; ⊙10am-10pm Sun-Wed, 10am-midnight Thu-Sat; Ⓜ Damac) may not rank among the city's megamalls, yet the shops are just as good and you won't get lost quite so readily. Browse global chains such as H&M, Reebok, Mango, Boots, Mothercare and the Early Learning Centre or stock up on goodies at the upmarket UK supermarket chain Waitrose. Several restaurants and cafes provide pit stops during store hopping.

❺ Market Marvels

From Wednesday to Saturday, the lively **Marina Market** (www.marinamarket. ae; ⊙10am-10pm Wed, to 11pm Thu-Sat; Ⓜ Damac) sets up on the promenade behind the Dubai Marina Mall and delivers clothing, handicrafts and unusual gift items galore. Look for Turkish hammam towels, upcycled handbags and handmade necklaces.

❻ Gourmet Tower

The circular, seven-story **Pier 7** (Marina Walk) is a feast for foodies with each floor holding a hip restaurant or bar with terraces delivering stunning views of bobbing yachts and twinkling towers. Options include gourmet comfort food at Fümé, sizzling Asian at Asia Asia and rooftop cocktails at Atelier M.

❼ Seafood Feast

Empty tables are a rare sight at **Barracuda** (☎04-452 2278; www.barracuda restaurant.net; Marina Walk; mains Dh85-205; ⊙noon-11.30pm; 🛜; Ⓜ Jumeirah Lakes Tower), an Egyptian seafood shrine where you pick your '*poisson*' (mullet, sea bream, pomfret) from the ice display and have it prepared any number of ways. The classic is oven-grilled and drizzled with olive oil and lemon. The large promenade-facing terrace offers *sheesha*-puffing and primo people-watching.

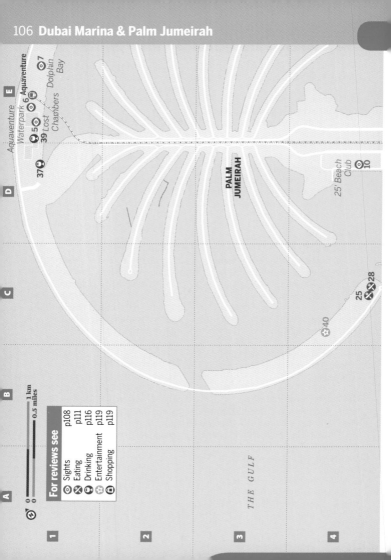

PALM JUMEIRAH

Aquaventure

Waterpark 6 **Aquaventure**

Dolphin
Bay

Lost
Chambers

25' Beach
Club

THE GULF

1 km
0.5 miles

For reviews see

Sights	p108
Eating	p111
Drinking	p116
Entertainment	p119
Shopping	p119

TECOM

32

Knowledge Village

DUBAI
INTERNET
CITY

Palm Jumeirah

Palm Jumeirah

Media City

18 29

38

15 One&Only
Spa

DUBAI
MEDIA CITY

33

Mina Al
Seyahi

30 9

Nakheel

Emirates
Golf
Club

DUBAI
MARINA

Club
Mina

Marina
Tower

Sheikh Zayed Rd

Interchange
No 5

21

24

35 17

Dubai
Marina

Skydive
Dubai

14

8

Zero
Gravity

Meydan
Beach
Club

11

22

1 The Walk at
JBR

Damac

Beach
Water
Park

4

JBR Open
Beach

3

41

42

Dubai
Jumeirah Beach
Residence 1

20 16

Favourite
Things

31 12

Dubai
Marina
Mall

The Beach
at JBR

34

27

2

26

36

23

Dubai
Ferry

13

Jumeirah
Lakes
Towers

Jumeirah Beach
Residence 2

19

Jumeirah
Lakes
Towers

Jumeirah Lakes
Towers

Sights

The Walk at JBR
NEIGHBOURHOOD

1 👁 Map p106, B6

In a city of air-conditioned malls, this attractive outdoor shopping and dining promenade was an immediate hit when it opened in 2008. Join locals and expats in strolling the 1.7km stretch, watching the world on parade from a pavement cafe, browsing the boutiques or ogling the Ferraris and other fancy cars cruising by on weekends. (Jumeirah Beach Residence; Ⓜ Jumeirah Lakes Towers, Damac, 🚋 Jumeirah Beach Residence 1 and 2)

The Beach at JBR
SHOPPING MALL

2 👁 Map p106, A6

Paralleling the beachfront for about 1km, the Beach at JBR is an open-plan cluster of low-lying buildings with wrapped around breezy squares and plazas. Restaurants with alfresco terraces dominate, although there are also a few shops thrown into the mix. Facing the ocean are a spongy running track, an outdoor gym, grassy areas and an open-air cinema. It's between the Hilton and Sheraton hotels. (www.thebeach.ae; The Walk at JBR; Ⓜ Jumeirah Lakes Towers, Damac, 🚋 Jumeirah Beach Residence 1 and 2)

JBR Open Beach
BEACH

3 👁 Map p106, B6

This clean and wonderful outdoor playground comes with plenty of facilities, including showers, toilets and changing rooms housed in distinctive panelled pods. Kids can keep cool in a splash zone or an offshore water park. Since it's right next to the Beach at JBR and the Walk at JBR, there's no shortage of food and drink outlets, although alcohol is only available in the hotels. (Jumeirah Beach Residence; admission free; Ⓜ Jumeirah Beach Residence 1 and 2)

Beach Water Park
WATER PARK

4 👁 Map p106, A6

This colourful, bouncy playground floats in the Gulf 150m off the Beach at JBR outdoor mall and consists of inflatable slides, jumping platforms, climbing walls, trampolines, balance beams and other fun features. (www.arabian waterparks.com; JBR Open Beach; per hour adult/child 6-11yr Dh60/50, day pass Dh195; ⏱8am-6pm; Ⓜ Jumeirah Lakes Towers)

Lost Chambers
AQUARIUM

5 👁 Map p106, E1

This fantastic labyrinth of underwater halls, passageways and fish tanks recreates the legend of the lost city of Atlantis. Some 65,000 exotic marine creatures inhabit 20 aquariums, where rays flutter and jellyfish dance, moray eels lurk and pretty-but-poisonous lionfish float. The centrepiece is the Ambassador Lagoon. For an extra fee you can snorkel or dive with the fishes in this 11.5-million-litre tank. (📞04-426 1040; Atlantis The Palm, Palm Jumeirah; general entry adult/child 6-11yr Dh100/70; ⏱10am-10pm; Monorail Aquaventure)

Aquaventure Waterpark

Aquaventure Waterpark

WATER PARK

6 ◉ Map p106, E1

Adrenalin rushes are guaranteed at this waterpark at the Atlantis The Palm resort. A 1.6km-long 'river' with rapids, wave surges and waterfalls meanders through the vast grounds that are anchored by two towers. The ziggurat-shaped Tower of Neptune is the launchpad for three slides, including the aptly named Leap of Faith, a near-vertical plunge into a shark-infested lagoon. (🅙04-426 0000; www. atlantisthepalm.com; Atlantis The Palm; over/under 120cm Dh250/205; ◷10am-sunset; 👣; Monorail Aquaventure)

Dolphin Bay

DOLPHIN PARK

7 ◉ Map p106, E1

Dolphin Bay offers a range of interactive experiences with bottlenose dolphins. Animal welfare groups say that keeping marine life in captivity is harmful and stressful, exacerbated further by human interaction. (🅙04-426 1030; www.atlantisthepalm.com; Atlantis The Palm; shallow-/deep-water interaction Dh795/960; ◷10am-6pm, varies seasonally; 👣; Monorail Aquaventure)

Zero Gravity

BEACH CLUB

8 ◉ Map p106, B6

Keep an eye on the Dubai Marina skyline and the daredevils jumping out of planes at this sleek beach club–bar next to the Drop Zone of SkyDubai, then cap a day of chilling and swimming with a night of drinks, snacks and international DJs. Fridays bring the Onshore Social, a late brunch running from 3pm to 6pm. (⏴04-399 0009; www.0-gravity.ae; Al Seyahi St, Skydive Dubai Drop Zone; day pass weekday/weekend Dh150/250, incl Dh50/100 food & beverage; ⏱9am-12.30am Sat-Wed, to 3am Thu & Fri; Ⓜ Damac)

Club Mina
BEACH CLUB

9 ◉ Map p106, C6

Set along 500m of private beach, this club is a joint venue of the Westin and Le Meridien Mina Seyahi beach resorts and gets a big thumbs up from families for its five pools (two

Local Life
Nostalgic Cruising

Tour Dubai (Map p106, B6; ⏴04-336 8407; www.tour-dubai.com; Marina Walk, near bridge; tours adult/child Dh130/90, dinner cruises Dh225/125; Ⓜ Damac) offers one-hour sightseeing tours on a historic dhow from the docks near the Barracuda restaurant. You'll be showered with prerecorded English commentary while taking in the sights and chilling on colourful upholstered benches. There are five tours daily between 10.30am and 5.30pm. In the evening, the dhows set sail for a two-hour dinner buffet with taped music. Alcohol is available.

covered ones for kids), a kids club and a watersports centre. Nice touch for grown-ups: cocktails in the swim-up bar. (⏴04-318 1420; www.lermeridien -minaseyahi.com; Le Meridien Mina Seyahi Beach Resort, Al-Sufouh Rd; day pass weekday/weekend Dh225/350; Ⓜ Nahkeel)

25' Beach Club
BEACH CLUB

10 ◉ Map p106, D4

Views back at the mainland are one of the most memorable aspects of a day at this family-oriented club at the swish Fairmont Hotel. Parents get to wiggle their toes in the sand or by the pool while the little ones let off steam in the Fairmont Faclon Juniors' Club with activities and playstations for toddlers to teens. (⏴04-457 3388; www.fairmont.com/palm-dubai; Fairmont The Palm, Palm Jumeirah; day pass weekday/weekend adult Dh200/250, child Dh150; Ⓜ Nakheel)

Meydan Beach Club
BEACH CLUB

11 ◉ Map p106, B6

Teeming with buff and bronzed bods, this stylish shoreline retreat near Dubai Marina has you stretching out on comfy white loungers surrounding a deep-blue infinity pool with floating sunbeds. There's a lounge for chilling with a cocktail and a spa for being pummelled into a state of blissfulness. (⏴04-433 3777; www.meydanbeach.com; The Walk at JBR; day pass weekday/weekend Dh150/250; ⏱10am-1am; Ⓜ Damac)

Favourite Things   ACTIVITY CENTRE

12 👁 Map p106, B7

This is one of the best and most popular indoor playgrounds for children up to age seven in town. It has a wide variety of stimulating environments to get busy, learn, role play and make new friends, including an art studio, a race track and a fancy dress room. (☎04-434 1984; www.favouritethings.com; 2nd fl, Dubai Marina Mall; ☺9am-9pm; 👶; Ⓜ Damac)

Dubai Ferry   BOAT TOUR

13 👁 Map p106, A6

Dubai Ferry runs several minicruises from its landing docks near the Dubai Marina Mall. There are daily departures at 11am, 1pm and 6.30pm up the coast all the way to the Al Ghubaiba docks on Dubai Creek, passing by Madinat Jumeirah, the Burj Al Arab, the World islands and the port in a 90-minute one-way trip. (☎800 9090; www.rta.ae; gold/silver ticket Dh75/50; Ⓜ Damac)

Skydive Dubai   SKYDIVING

14 👁 Map p106, B6

Daredevils can experience the rush of jumping out of a plane and soaring above the Dubai skyline by signing up for these tandem parachute flights. The minimum age is 18; weight and height restrictions apply as well. (☎04-377 8888; www.skydivedubai.ae; Skydive Dr, Dubai Marina; tandem jump, video & photos Dh2000; ☺8am-4pm Mon-Sat; Ⓜ Damac)

One&Only Spa   SPA

15 👁 Map p106, D6

Do you want to unwind, restore or elevate? These are the magic words at this exclusive spa with a dozen treatment rooms where massages, wraps, scrubs and facials are calibrated to achieve your chosen goal. Staff can help find the perfect massage or wrap for whatever ails you, although you can never go wrong with a session in the Oriental Hammam. (☎04-315 2140; http://royalmirage.oneandonlyresorts.com; One&Only Royal Mirage, Al Sufouh Rd; ☺9.30am-9pm, women only until 1pm; Ⓜ Nakheel)

Eating

Fümé   INTERNATIONAL $$

16 🍴 Map p106, B6

With its funky design elements, relaxed crew and crowd, and rustic comfort food, Fümé brings more than a touch of urban cool to the Marina. The menu is casual enough not to intimidate yet endowed with plenty of creative dishes to keep foodies happy. Bestseller: the superjuicy beef chuck ribs roasted for six hours in a closed charcoal oven. No reservations. (☎04-421 5669; www.fume-eatery.com; Pier 7; mains Dh55-95; ☺noon-2am; Ⓜ Damac, Dubai Marina Mall)

Indego by Vineet   INDIAN $$$

17 🍴 Map p106, C6

India's first Michelin-starred chef, Vineet Bhatia, is the man behind the menu at what many consider Dubai's top Indian restaurant. Though gorgeous, the intimate dining room – lorded over by big brass Natraj sculptures – is still eclipsed by such exquisite dishes as house-smoked salmon, wild mushroom biryani and chocolate samosas. Great brunch, too. (☑04-317 6000; www.indegobyvineet.com; ground fl, Tower 1, Grosvenor House, Al Sufouh Rd; mains Dh125-310, brunch with/without alcohol Dh350/250; ⊙lunch & dinner; ⊠Damac, ⊠Jumeirah Beach Residence 1)

Tagine
MOROCCAN **$$**

18 🍴 Map p106, D6

Get cosy between throw pillows at a low-slung table in the seductively lit dining room, then treat your taste buds while tapping your toes to the live Moroccan duo. Fez-capped waiters serve big platters of couscous and tajines (stew cooked in a clay pot) with all the extras, including a vegetarian choice. The cumin-laced roast lamb shoulder is another fine menu pick. (☑04-399 9999; http://royalmirage.oneandonlyresorts. com; The Palace, One&Only Royal Mirage, Al Sufouh Rd; tagine Dh105; ⊙7pm-11.30pm Tue-Sun; ⊠Dubai Internet City, ⊠Media City)

Aquara
SEAFOOD **$$$**

19 🍴 Map p106, A7

The views of fancy yachts and a forest of sleek high-rises impress almost as much as the Asian-infused fare at this chic seafood shrine serving dock-fresh ingredients and flawlessly crafted plates. There's lots of special events,

such as a Caribbean barbecue on Saturday afternoons, a British roast on Saturday nights and a Friday evening brunch. (☑04-362 7900; www.dubai marinayachtclub.com; Dubai Marina Yacht Club, Marina Walk; mains Dh95-200; ⊙6.30pm-midnight; ⊠Jumeirah Lakes Towers)

Asia Asia
FUSION **$$$**

20 🍴 Map p106, B6

Prepare for a culinary journey along the ancient Spice Route as you enter this gorgeous restaurant via a candle-lit corridor that spills into an exotic booth-lined lounge with dangling bird-cage lamps. The menu blends Asian and Middle Eastern flavours, usually with finesse and success. The sambal chicken tajine, Persian black cod and Peking duck are signature dishes. Full bar. (☑04-276 5900; 6th fl, Pier 7; mains Dh70-180; ⊙4pm-midnight; ⊠Damac)

Toro Toro
SOUTH AMERICAN **$$**

21 🍴 Map p106, C6

The decor packs as much pizazz as the food at this pan-Latin outpost conceived by star chef Richard Sandoval. Opt for the *rodizio* menu (a free-flow of grilled meats carved at your table) or put together a meal from small-plate dishes: lamb shank in adobo sauce, salmon ceviche or grilled octopus are among top picks. Great rum and cachaca selections. (☑04-317 6000; www.torotoro-dubai.com; ground fl, Tower 2, Grosvenor House; small plates Dh60-130; ⊙7.30pm-2am Sat-Wed, to

IAIN MASTERTON / ALAMY ©

Monorail to Palm Jumeirah

3am Thu & Fri; M Damac, 🚶 Jumeirah Beach Residence 1)

Eauzone
INTERNATIONAL $$$

This jewel of a restaurant (see **18** ⊗ Map p106, D6) is an inspired port of call drawing friends, romancing couples and fashionable families to a sublime setting with shaded decks jutting out over illuminated pools. The Asian focus of the lunch menu is supplemented by European accents at dinnertime. Try the seared scallops, herb-crusted sea bass or twice-cooked duck. (☎04-399 9999; http://royalmirage. oneandonlyresorts.com; Arabian Court, One&Only Royal Mirage, Al Sufouh Rd; mains lunch Dh65-170, dinner Dh135-250; ⊙lunch & dinner; 🛜; M Nakheel, 🚶 Media City)

Maya
MEXICAN $$$

22 ⊗ Map p106, B6

Richard Sandoval, the man who introduced modern Mexican food to the US, is behind the menu at this sophisticated restaurant where you'll be treated to a piñata of flavours. Start out with creamy guacamole, prepared tableside of course, before moving on to such succulent mains as *mole poblano* (chicken with chilli and chocolate sauce), tequila chipotle prawns or sizzling chicken fajitas. Lovely rooftop lounge as well. (☎04-316 5550; www. maya-dubai.com; Le Royal Meridien Beach Resort & Spa, Al Sufouh Rd; mains Dh80-230; ⊙dinner Mon-Sat; M Damac, 🚶 Jumeirah Beach Residence 1)

Understand

Pitfalls in Paradise

Even in a city known for its audacious megaprojects, the Palm Jumeirah pushes the limits of innovation: a huge artificial island in the shape of a palm tree. It is an extraordinary feat of engineering, especially when considering that only natural materials – rock and sand – were used in its construction.

Built to almost double Dubai's existing 72km of coastline, it consists of a 2km trunk and a 16-frond crown protected by an 11km-long crescent-shaped breakwater. An elevated driverless monorail whisks passengers from the bottom of the trunk (where it links with the Dubai Tram) to the Atlantis The Palm Hotel, the first of several giant resorts to be completed. In recent years, it has been joined by a few others, including the One&Only The Palm, the Waldorf Astoria, the Jumeirah Zabeel Saray, the Kempinksi and the Rixos The Palm.

Perhaps not surprisingly, the daring and unprecedented construction of a vast island has resulted in a number of problems and challenges. Delayed completion and residents disgruntled by the increased construction density and lower building quality were only the beginning. A bigger problem turned out to be the breakwater. The original continuous crescent prevented natural tidal movement, leading to stagnant seawater, excessive algae growth and smelly beaches. Now that two 100m-wide gaps have been cut out of the crescent the problem appears to have been solved.

An ongoing issue, though, is the erosion of Dubai's sandy mainland beaches. Building the giant island so close to the shoreline changed the wave movement and diverted the natural current, which is affecting the outline of the shore. In some areas sand is deposited, in others the beach is eroded by up to 10m per year, threatening roads and resorts if left unchecked. Experts expect that over time the coastline will settle down, but in the meantime, replacing the eroded sand is a costly and Sisyphean process.

Another study reported that The Palm is actually sinking by a clip of 5mm per year, but the developer Nakheel has categorically refuted the claim.

BiCE

ITALIAN $$$

23 Map p106, A6

This restaurant has a pedigree going back to 1930s Milan. That was when Beatrice 'Bice' Ruggeri first opened her trattoria, which by the 1970s had become one of the city's most fashionable. Today, Dubai's BiCE carries on the tradition with chef Cosimo adding his creative touch to such traditional dishes as oven-baked sea bass and veal tenderloin with foie gras sauce. (04-318 2520; Hilton Dubai Jumeirah, The Walk at JBR; pasta Dh80-125, mains Dh170-245; 12.30-11.30pm Sat-Thu, 1-11.30pm Fri; Jumeirah Lakes Towers, Jumeirah Beach Residence 1, Jumeirah Beach Residence 2)

Rhodes W1

MODERN BRITISH $$$

24 Map p106, C6

Michelin-decorated chef Gary Rhodes is famous for bringing British cuisine into the 21st century. At this revamped Dubai outpost, his dedication to revolutionising humble classics such as shepherd's pie, rack of lamb and roast cod into sophisticated, zeitgeist-capturing dishes shines brightly. (04-317 6000; www.rw1-dubai.com; Grosvenor House, Al Sufouh Rd; mains Dh95-190; 7-11pm; Damac, Jumeirah Beach Residence 1)

101 Lounge & Bar

MEDITERRANEAN $$$

25 Map p106, C4

With to-die-for views of the Marina high-rises, it may be hard to concentrate on the food at this buzzy marina-adjacent pavilion at the ultraswish One&Only The Palm resort. Come for nibbles and cocktails in the bar or go for the full dinner experience (paella, grills, pastas). Ask about the free boat shuttle when making reservations. (04-440 1030; thepalm.oneandonlyresorts.com; West Crescent, One&Only The Palm; mains Dh85-220, tapas selection of 3/6/9 Dh90/160/220; 11am-1am)

Massaad

LEBANESE $$

26 Map p106, A6

All the usual Lebanese mezze and grills are accounted for at this teensy country-style eatery. Most of the fresh ingredients – from lemons to chickens – are sourced from growers based in nearby Al Ain. Specialities include the rolled pita chicken sandwiches and fingerlickin' *shish tawooq* (marinated chicken grilled on skewers) served on a traditional wooden board called *tablieh*. (04-362 9002; www.massaadfarmtotable.com; ground fl, Amwaj block, The Walk at JBR; mains Dh36-70; 10am-4am; Jumeirah Lakes Towers, Jumeirah Beach Residence 2)

Sushi Art

JAPANESE $$

27 Map p106, A6

Sushi purist or not, you're sure to find your favourite among the huge, attractive selection at this minimalist cafe. The most enticing morsels are those designed by French Michelin chef Joël Robuchon and include a swoon-worthy crispy lobster roll that goes well with a crunchy, sesame-infused seaweed salad. (800 220;

www.sushiart.ae; The Beach at JBR; nigiri Dh25-42, maki per piece Dh7-22; ⏱11am-midnight; Ⓜ Jumeirah Lakes Towers, 🚇 Jumeirah Beach Residence 2)

Stay
FRENCH $$$

28 Map p106, C4

Triple-Michein-starred Yannick Alléno introduces his culinary magic to Dubai in this vaulted dining room accented with black crystal chandeliers. His creations seem deceptively simple (the beef tenderloin with fries and black pepper sauce is a bestseller), letting the superb ingredients shine brightly. An unexpected stunner is the Pastry Library, an entire wall of sweet treats. (☎04-440 1030; http://thepalm.oneandonly resorts.com; Western Crescent, One&Only The Palm; mains Dh190-300; ⏱dinner)

Drinking

Jetty Lounge
BAR, LOUNGE

29 Map p106, D6

From the moment you start following the meandering path through the One&Only's luxuriant gardens, you'll sense that you're heading for a pretty special place. Classy without the pretence, Jetty Lounge is all about unwinding (preferably at sunset) on plush white sofas scattered right in the sand. There's a full bar menu and snacks for nibbling. (☎04-399 9999; www.royalmirage.oneandonlyresorts.com; The Palace, One&Only Royal Mirage, Al Sufouh Rd; ⏱2pm-late; 🛜; Ⓜ Nakheel)

Barasti
BAR

30 Map p106, C6

Beachside Barasti is primarily a Brit-expat favourite for lazy days on the beach and is often jam-packed with shiny happy party people knocking back the brewskis. There's soccer and rugby on the big screen, a deck with pool tables, occasional bands and drinks specials on Monday nights. (☎04-399 3333; www.barastibeach.com; Le Meridien Mina Seyahi Beach Resort, Dubai Marina, Al Sufouh Rd; ⏱11am-1.30am Sat-Wed, to 3am Thu & Fri; Ⓜ Nakheel)

Atelier M
BAR, CLUB

31 Map p106, A7

Atelier M is a three-floor treat atop the circular Pier 7 building. The lift drops you at the restaurant which serves inspired French-Asian dinners best enjoyed on the wraparound terrace with views of the twinkling Dubai Marina. A spiralling staircase leads up to the bar looking splendid in futuristic art deco. (☎04-450 7766; www. atelierm.ae; Pier 7; Ⓜ Damac)

Basement
CLUB

32 Map p106, E8

The antithesis of the see-and-be-seen glamour vibe, Basement is about as underground as things get in Dubai. It draws dedicated clubbers to parties hosted by different promoters and featuring both local and visiting DJ talent playing a soundscape from house and funk to dancehall. (☎04-434 5555;

IAIN MASTERTON / ALAMY ©

Camels on the beach at Dubai Marina

www.boutique7.ae; Boutique 7 Hotel & Suites, Tecom; ⏱10pm-3am; Ⓜ Dubai Internet City)

Dek on 8
BAR

33 Map p106, C7

Mingle with media types beside the pool at this alfresco chill zone on the 8th floor of the Media One Hotel. On weekends, beat junkies press flesh on the dance floor, then refuel with bar bites while reclined on leather sofas and lounge beds.

The Thursday happy hour (5pm to 8pm) is perfect for ringing in the weekend with Dh33 drinks. (☎04-427 1000; www.mediaonehotel.com; Media One Hotel; ⏱noon-midnight; Ⓜ Nakheel)

Bliss Lounge
BAR

34 Map p106, A6

Feel the breeze in your hair as you stake out your turf at the circular bar or on a cushiony sofa at this beachfront bar just off the Walk at JBR. Resident DJs play deep house for dedicated chilling with cocktails and eye-candy. Sushi and tapas dominate the menu. (☎04-315 3886; www.blissloungedubai.com; Sheraton Jumeirah Beach Resort, Al Sufouh Rd; ⏱noon-3am; 🛜; Ⓜ Jumeirah Lakes Towers)

Siddharta
BAR, LOUNGE

35 Map p106, C6

Part of Buddha Bar in the same hotel, Siddharta is an urban oasis and a great spot to join Dubai's glam crowd

Top Tip

Dubai Tram

The Dubai Marina is one of the most pedestrian-friendly areas in town and also has some convenient public transport. One way to get from A to B is aboard the brand-new air-conditioned Dubai Tram that trundles between Dubai Internet City and the Jumeirah Beach Residences.

in taking the party from daytime by the pool to night-time basking in the glow of the Marina high-rises. Nice music, expertly mixed cocktails and swift service make up for the rather steep price tab. (☑04-399 8888; Tower 2, Grosvenor House, Al Sufouh Rd; ⊙10am-1pm Sat-Wed, to 2am Thu & Fri; ⓂDamac)

Pure Sky Lounge
BAR

36 Map p106, A6

When it comes to glorious views over the beach and Palm Jumeirah, this chic indoor-outdoor lounge is in a lofty league on the 35th floor of the beachfront Hilton. White wicker chairs and lounges accented with turquoise pillows channel a chill, maritime mood. Half-price cocktails during happy hour (5pm to 7pm). (☑04-399 1111; Hilton Dubai Jumeirah Resort, The Walk at JBR; ⊙5pm-2am; ⓂDamac)

Maya Lounge
BAR

Arrive an hour before sunset to snag one of the Gulf-view tables on the rooftop bar of this upmarket Mexican

restaurant (see 22 ⊗ Map p106, B6) and swill top-shelf margaritas as the sun slowly slips into the sea. On Señorita Sunday ladies can score three free drinks between 7pm and 1am. (☑04-316 5550; www.maya-dubai.com; Le Royal Meridien Beach Resort & Spa, Al Sufouh Rd; ⊙6pm-2am Mon-Sat; ⓂDamac)

Nasimi Beach
BEACH CLUB

37 Map p106, D1

This beach club at the Atlantis caters to hip and libidinous party animals (no kids allowed) working on their tan sprawled on a double sunbed while being showered with house, funk and electro. The vibe picks up in the afternoon, especially on weekends when happy hour runs from 5pm to 7pm. (☑04-426 2626; www.atlantistheplan.com; West Beach, Atlantis The Palm; minimum spend weekday/weekend Dh150/250; ⊙11am-midnight Sun-Thu, to 1am Fri & Sat; Monorail Aquaventure)

Rooftop Terrace & Sports Lounge
BAR

With its fabric-draped nooks, cushioned banquettes, Moroccan lanterns and Oriental carpets, this lounge (see 18 ⊗ Map p106, D6) is one of Dubai's classiest sports bars. Catch live games in the circular bar, then report to the rooftop for chilling under the stars. There's also a good menu of mezze, in case you're feeling peckish. (☑04-399 9999; http://royalmirage.oneandonlyresorts.com; Arabian Court, One&Only Royal Mirage, Al Sufouh Rd; ⊙5pm-1am; 🛜; ⓂNakheel)

Tamanya Terrace   BAR, SHEESHA

38 Map p106, D7

On the eighth floor of the Radisson, this is a fab spot for kicking off a long night of partying with sundowners against the backdrop of the forest of sparkling Marina skyscrapers. Mod furnishings, sassy lighting and international DJs fuel the vibe. (04-366 9111; www.radissonblu.com/hotel-mediacity dubai; Radisson Blu Hotel, Dubai Media City; 5pm-2am Sun-Thu, 6pm-2am Fri & Sat; ; Nakheel)

N'Dulge   CLUB

39 Map p106, E1

Headlining DJs rock the Arena, the centrepiece dance floor of this sexy nightclub where magicians, mimes, dancers and stilt walkers perform on a circular suspended catwalk. For a chill interlude, head to the Lounge for drinks, a bite and deep house or to the Terrace for sushi, *sheesha* and house with an Arabian twist. (04-426 0561; www.atlantisthepalm.com; Atlantis The Palm; 9.30pm-3am; Monorail Aquaventure)

Entertainment

Music Hall   LIVE MUSIC

40 Map p106, C4

It's not a theatre, not a club, not a bar and not a restaurant – MusicHall is all those things. The concept hails from Beirut where it's had audiences clapping since 2003 with an eclectic line-up of live music – from Indian to country, and rock to Russian ballads. The food, however, is an afterthought (minimum spend). (056-270 8670; www.jumeirah.com; Jumeirah Zabeel Saray; mains Dh180-290; 9pm-3am Thu & Fri)

Shopping

Boutique 1   FASHION

41 Map p106, B6

Ground zero for prêt-à-porter straight off the runways of Paris and Milan, Boutique 1 feeds Dubai's fashion cravings with the latest from classic and avant-garde designers from around the globe. Its gorgeous three-storey store on the Walk at JB stocks not only fashionable frocks but also home accessories, beauty products, furniture and books. (04-425 7888; www.boutique1.com; The Walk at JBR; 10am-11pm; Jumeirah Lakes Towers)

Gallery One   ART & STATIONERY

42 Map p106, B6

If you love art but can't afford an original, pick up a highly decorative print by well-known Middle Eastern artists without breaking the bank. Some motifs are also available as greetings cards, posters, notebooks and calendars. (04-423 1987; www.g-1.com; The Walk at JBR; 10am-10pm; Jumeirah Lakes Towers)

Local Life
Let's Do Brunch...

Friday brunch is a major element of the Dubai social scene and just about every hotel-restaurant in town sets up an all-you-can-eat buffet with an option for unlimited wine or bubbly. Some indie eateries also do brunch but without alcohol. Here are our top pig-out picks in town. Bookings are essential.

❶ The Motherlode
Expect to loosen your belt after enjoying the cornucopia of delectables at the **Al Qasr Friday Brunch** (☎04-366 6730; Al Qasr Hotel, Madinat Jumeirah; soft drinks/alcohol/champagne Dh475/575/795; ⏰12.30-4pm Fri; Ⓜ Mall of the Emirates). Feast on roast lamb, sushi, cooked-to-order seafood, foie gras, salads, mezze, all sorts of hot dishes, plus an entire cheese room. The selection is so huge, guests get a map to find their way around.

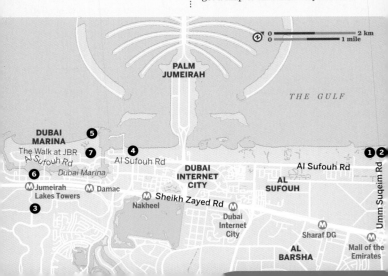

2 Family-Friendly Feast

Three restaurants – Tortuga (Mexican), Al Muna (Arabian) and Zheng He's (Chinese) – pull out all the stops at the epic **Grand Friday Brunch** (📞04-366 6730; Mina A' Salam Hotel, Madinat Jumeirah; with/without alcohol Dh525/425; ⏰12.30-4pm Fri; 👶; Ⓜ Mall of the Emirates) at the Mina A' Salam Hotel, with dreamy views of the Burj Al Arab from coveted water-front tables. Pace yourself while tucking into fajitas, sushi, barbecued shrimp and other delish dishes while a band belts out popular hits. Turtle feeding at 1pm and a supervised play area give this brunch an edge with families.

3 Jazz Brunch

The cheap and cheerful brunch at **Jazz@PizzaExpress** (📞04-441 6342; www.pizzaexpressuae.com; Cluster A, Jumeirah Lakes Towers, Dubai Marina; with/without alcohol Dh189/99; ⏰noon-4pm Fri; Ⓜ Jumeirah Lakes Towers) has you filling up on Italian faves – antipasti, pasta, thin-crust pizza – ordered à la carte and brought to your table. Live jazz sets the mood.

4 International Indulgence

Bubbalicious (Al Sufouh Rd, Dubai Marina; soft drinks/house drinks/sparkling wine Dh390/490/650; ⏰1-4pm Fri; Ⓜ Nakheel) is the culinary bonanza orchestrated by three of the Westin Dubai Mina Seyahi restaurants: the family-friendly Blue Orange, the Hunters Room & Grill steakhouse and the Asia-flavoured Spice Emporium. Highlights are the 10 cooking stations and the above-average cheese selection.

5 Afternoon Revelry

The perfect brunch for sleepyheads, the **Onshore Social** (📞04-399 0009; www.0-gravity.ae; Al Seyahi St, Skydive Dubai Drop Zone; Dh444, with champagne Dh666; ⏰3-6pm Fri; Ⓜ Damac) at the Zero Gravity beach club doesn't kick into gear until the afternoon, taking revellers from day to night amid an avalanche of global faves, from dim sum to antipasti and lamb chops to decadent desserts. Stay on for sunset and night-time DJ beats.

6 Brunch under the Stars

If guzzling free-flowing champagne at midday isn't your thing, hit the evening buffet at **Aquara** (📞04-362 7900; Aquara, Dubai Marina Yacht Club, Dubai Marina; with soft/house/premium drinks Dh220/350/400; ⏰7.30-10.30pm Fri; Ⓜ Jumeirah Lakes Towers) to expand your waistline while chilling with a view of the sparkling Dubai Marina. Tantalise your tummy with a gorgeous smorgasbord that's especially strong on fish and seafood.

7 Carnivorous Delight

Fans of churrasco grills will be in heaven at the **Hola Hola brunch** (📞04-317 6000; www.torotoro-dubai.com; Grosvenor House, Al Sufouh Rd; with/without alcohol Dh500/350; ⏰12.30-4pm Fri; Ⓜ Damac; 🚊Jumeirah Beach Residence 1) at Toro Toro, a sassy Latin American outpost at the Grosvenor House. Offering the regular menu's most popular dishes (including creamy guacamole and toothsome ceviche), this brunch is a great way to sample celebrity chef Richard Sandoval's culinary concoctions.

Top Sights
Abu Dhabi

Getting There

🚌 Depart several times hourly from Dubai's Al Ghubaiba station in Bur Dubai (single/return Dh25/50, two hours).

🚕 Cabbies charge around Dh250 each way.

About 150km south of Dubai, the emirate of Abu Dhabi sits atop the world's fourth-largest oil reserves, but does not flaunt its wealth quite as brazenly as its neighbour. However, in recent years it too has built up a portfolio of attractions, sharpening its profile as an increasingly popular tourist destination of its own. The key project is a new Cultural District on Saadiyat Island designed by international starchitects, including branches of the Louvre and the Guggenheim art museums.

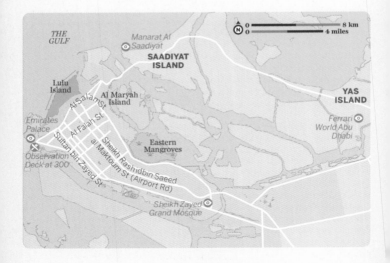

Don't Miss

Grand Mosque

With 82 marble domes and four 107m-high minarets shaping its silhouette, the **Sheikh Zayed Grand Mosque** (☎02-441 6444; www.szgmc.ae; 2nd Sheikh Rashid bin Saeed al Maktoum St; admission free; ⏰9am-10pm Sat-Thu, 4.30-11pm Fri) is a masterpiece of modern Islamic architecture and design. It can accommodate up to 40,000 worshippers and is a decorative symphony of marble, gold, semi-precious stones and crystals.

Emirates Palace

No need to check-in to check out the **Emirates Palace** (☎02-690 9000; www.emiratespalace.com; Corniche Rd West), one of the world's most expensive hotels ever built – a cool US$6 billion. The interior is an opulent feast decked out in marble, gold and mother of pearl, with palm trees and over 1000 Swarovski crystal chandeliers.

Saadiyat Cultural District

Taking shape on Saadiyat Island, this cultural district is an artistic oasis that will include outposts of the Guggenheim and the Louvre, a museum dedicated to UAE founding father Sheikh Zayed and a performing arts centre. Visit the high-tech exhibit at **Manarat Al Saadiyat** (☎02-657 5800; www.saadiyat.ae; Cultural District; admission free; ⏰9am-8pm) to get a sense of the vision and scope of the project.

Ferrari World Abu Dhabi

A must for speed freaks, **Ferrari World** (☎02-496 8000; www.ferrariworldabudhabi.com; Yas Island; adult/child under 1.3m Dh250/205, premium admission Dh450/365; ⏰11am-8pm, varies with the seasons) on Yas Island is a temple of torque that's home to the world's fastest roller coaster plus tamer diversions such as a V12 engine flume ride, motion-simulators and antique cars.

☑ Top Tips

▶ To get your bearings, consider a trip on the hop-on, hop-off **Big Bus Abu Dhabi** (☎02-449 0026; www.bigbustours.com; 24hr adult/child Dh200/100, 48hr adult/child Dh260/130; ⏰9am-7pm).

▶ Take a free guided tour of the Grand Mosque, which includes a Q&A (in English).

✕ Take a Break

Enjoy English-style high tea, coffee or mocktails backed by a sweeping panorama at **Observation Deck at 300** (☎02-811 5666; www.jumeirah.com; Tower 2, Level 74, Jumeirah at Etihad Towers; entry Dh75, incl Dh50 for food or drink, high tea Dh175; ⏰10am-6pm) on the 74th floor of the Jumeirah at Etihad Towers hotel.

Try a Palace Cappuccino at the Emirates Palace: sprinkled with 24-carat gold flakes, it's the ultimate in delicious decadence.

The Best of
Dubai

Dubai Marina at night
NIKADA / CORBIS ©

Best Walks
Deira Souq Stroll

🏃 The Walk

The Deira souq area is one of the most historic and atmospheric districts in Dubai and is best explored by foot. It's a bustling, nicely chaotic warren of lanes teeming with exotic stalls and shops and especially bustling in the evenings. Our tour covers the main bazaars and also incorporates a couple of heritage stops into its route.

Start Spice Souq; *abra* station Deira Old Souq

Finish Covered Souq; Ⓜ Baniyas Square

Length 2km; three hours

🍴 Take a Break

Wrap up a ramble around Deira's souqs with a carnivorous feast at the **Afghan Khorasan Kebab House** (☎ 04-234 0999; off Deira St, near Naif Mosque; mains Dh22-39; ⏰ noon-1am; Ⓜ Baniyas Sq). Eat with your hands and sit upstairs in the carpeted *majlis* (meeting room). It's located in an alley behind Naif Mosque, off Deira St.

PETER UNGER / LONELY PLANET IMAGES ©

Souq in Deira

❶ Spice Souq

As soon as you step off the *abra* (traditional wooden ferry), heady scents will lure you across to the **Spice Souq** (p28). The guttural singsong of Arabic bounces around the lanes of this small covered market where stall-holders hawk everything from medicinal herbs to exotic spices and frankincense.

❷ Heritage House

En route to the **Heritage House** (p28), you'll pass stores selling nuts, pulses and rice. The shops belong to wholesalers who trade mainly with Iran and use dhows to ply their goods. The house once belong to a pearl merchant and is a fine example of a classic Emirati family home; inside are exhibits on aspects of Dubai history and culture.

❸ Al Ahmadiya School

Head next door to duck inside the **Al Ahmadiya School** (p28), Dubai's oldest public school, founded by the very pearl merchant who once lived next door. It adjoins a petite square flanked by a heritage hotel, an old mosque and small shops.

❹ Gold Souq

Continue along Al Ahmadiya St, turning right into Old Baladiya St, where you'll find more wholesalers – this time trading in *gutras* (men's white headcloths), sandals and Chinese products. Ahead, to the left, you'll spot the entrance to the famous **Gold Souq**

(p24), whose shops are filled with everything from simple earrings to elaborate creations for bridal dowries.

❺ Perfume Souq

Exit the Gold Souq and follow Sikkat Al Khail St to Al Soor St and turn left. This is the heart of the **Perfume Souq** (p28), a string of shops selling heady Arabian *attars* (perfumes) and *oud* (fragrant wood). Backtrack and continue straight on what is now 107th St,

with hawkers selling cut-price clothes and kitschy souvenirs.

❻ Covered Souq

Tucked southeast of 107th St are the tiny alleys of the **Covered Souq** (p28), a labyrinth of little shops selling everything from textiles to *sheesha* (water pipes). It's one to poke around, watch the crowd haggle for deals and perhaps even ferret out the occasional useful bargain oneself.

Best Walks
Bur Dubai Waterfront Walk

🏃 The Walk

This heritage walk of Dubai's oldest area kicks off in the Al Fahidi Historic District, where you can wander around the atmospheric narrow lanes and peek into the renovated wind-tower houses. The route ticks off several of Dubai's most interesting traditional sights along the Creek and provides a glimpse into a bygone era with not a shopping mall, skyscraper or ski slope in sight.

Start Al Fahidi Historic District; Ⓜ Al Fahidi

Finish Shindagha Historic District; Ⓜ Al Ghubaiba

Length 3km; three to four hours

✕ Take a Break

With excellent views of the Creek, **Bait Al Wakeel** (☏ 04-353 0530; Bur Dubai Souq, waterfront; mezze Dh12-30, mains Dh35-120; ⏱ noon-11pm; Ⓜ Al Ghubaiba) serves Lebanese snacks, such as felafel and hummus, along with a range of fruit juices and teas.

THE DIVING VILLAGE

Entrance to the Diving Village (p48)

❶ Al Fahidi Historic District

Kick off your tour with a leisurely wander along the narrow lanes of one of Dubai's oldest **neighbourhoods** (p42) and check out the traditional wind-tower architecture. Pop into small museums such as the **Coffee Museum** or the **Al Serkal Cultural Foundation** and the flower-filled courtyards of **XVA** (p46), a cafe, gallery and gift shop, or the **Arabian Tea House** (p50).

❷ Dubai Museum

Wrap up the historic district by popping into the **Majlis Gallery** (p43), the oldest art space in Dubai, before continuing west along bustling Al Fahidi St to the **Dubai Museum** (p40). Spend about an hour soaking up the history, heritage and development of this burgeoning city. Turn left as you exit the museum and study the architectural details of the Grand Mosque topped by Dubai's tallest minaret.

❸ Hindi Lane

Take the lane to the mosque's right-hand side, and continue straight ahead for a few steps, then duck left into teensy **Hindi Lane** (p46), a vibrant and colourful alley with pint-sized stores selling religious paraphernalia to be offered in the upstairs temple. At the end of the lane, turn right and head to **Creekside Plaza**, which has picture-perfect views of the *abra* and dhow traffic.

❹ Bur Dubai Souq

Backtrack and turn right beneath the wooden arcades of the **Bur Dubai Souq** (p46) with its colourful textile and trinket shops. After arriving at the Bur Dubai *abra* station, follow the waterfront to the Shindagha Historic District, which is lined with the historic restored residences of Dubai's ruling family.

❺ Shindagha Historic District

Several of these residences now house themed exhibits, such as the **Camel Museum**

(p48) or the **Traditional Architecture Museum** (p47). The key building here, though, is the splendid **Sheikh Saeed Al Maktoum House** (p47), where exhibits include an intriguing collection of

historic photographs of Dubai. If you're visiting during Eid or the Dubai Shopping Festival, the **Heritage and Diving Villages** (p48) will be a hive of activity.

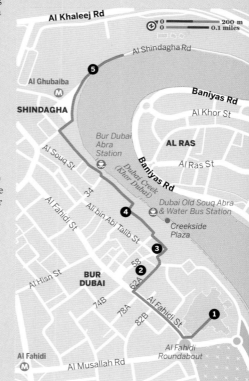

Best
Eating

Filling your tummy in Dubai is an extraordinarily multicultural experience with a virtual UN of cuisines to choose from. Lebanese and Indian fare are most prevalent, but basically you can feast on anything from Afghan kebabs to fish and chips in the city's myriad eateries. These run the gamut from simple street kitchens and fast-food franchises to family restaurants and luxe dining temples.

Local ingredients

Taking global fare local has arrived with a vengeance in Dubai. A new generation of chefs now lets the trio of 'seasonal-regional-organic' ingredients steer their menus, thereby adding pizazz to time-tested recipes and making them lighter, healthier and more creative. Many grow their own herbs or vegetables, pick up fresh produce from regional farmers and source their eggs in nearby Al Ain and their fish from the Gulf waters.

Food Trucks

The export hit from the US and the UK finally started rolling into Dubai in 2014. A growing crop of colourful mobile kitchens can be spotted throughout the city (p78), usually at parties, concerts, events or open-air markets, with exact dates and locations posted via social media.

Emirati cuisine

Restaurants serving Emirati food used to be rare, but thankfully this is changing. Traditional plates are rooted in the Bedouin diet and often consist of one-pot stews infused with cinnamon, saffron and turmeric and topped with nuts or dried fruit.

NICO TONDINI / GETTY IMAGES ©

☑ **Top Tips**

▶ Make weekend bookings for top tables, including Friday brunch, at least a week ahead.

▶ Only international hotel restaurants and a few independent venues are licensed to serve alcohol.

Best Cheap Eats

Al Tawasol Sit on the floor Bedouin-style and feast on Yemeni classics without cutlery. (p30)

Special Ostadi Sheikhs to shoe shiners clutter this funky been-here-forever Iranian kebab joint. (p50)

Ravi Empty tables are as rare as hen's teeth at this unfussy curry

Middle Eastern cuisine

temple with sidewalk seating. (p62)

Best Emirati

Milas Fresh juices complement the soulful goodness of updated local dishes. (p94)

Al Fanar This traditional lair is an ode to Emirati cuisine. (p62)

Best Middle Eastern

Aroos Damascus Seriously delicious Syrian staples swiftly served with a smile. (p31)

Samad Al Iraqi A top place to try Iraq's national dish, *mangouf* (woodfire-roasted fish). (p62)

Kan Zaman Terrific mezze, billowing *sheesha*

and sparkling Creek views. (p50)

Shabestan Persian cuisine fit for a royal with Creek views. (p30)

Best Indian

Indego by Vineet Michelin man Vineet Bhatia puts contemporary spins on Indian classics. (p111)

Jaffer Bhai's Sign up for a culinary audience with the self-proclaimed 'biryani king of Mumbai'. (p49)

Best for Romance

Pai Thai If your date doesn't make you swoon, these top Thai treats should still ensure an unforgettable evening. (p77)

Qbara A '10' on the romance-meter for its sensuous decor and matching modern Middle Eastern cuisine. (p49)

Pierchic The breezy pier setting, Burj Al Arab views and superb seafood pack this place to the gills. (p77)

Best Urban Hotspots

Tom & Serg This industrial-flavoured loft is a top stop on an Al Quoz gallery hop. (p72)

Zaroob Tasty Lebanese street food in a setting so perky it may get you off your meds. (p93)

Fümé Dubai Marina views are gratis at this rustic city slicker trading in global comfort food. (p111)

Best
Bars

Dubai may be famous for its glitzy-glam clubs, but of late it's also been growing a more low-key underground scene. The busiest nights are Thursday and Friday – Dubai's weekend nights – when party animals let off steam in bars and on the dance floor. Alcohol is served in hotels and some licensed venues only. Many Emiratis tend to prefer going out for *sheesha*, mocktails or coffee.

SARAH KASTNER / STOCK4B / GETTY IMAGES ©

Trends

Beachfront lounges and rooftop bars are all the rage these days, as is the supper club concept that wraps dining, drinking and dancing into one fabulous package. In the cooler months, some of the hottest parties don't wait for the moon to be high in the sky but start turning beach clubs into hedonistic cauldrons by the afternoon.

Happy Hours & Ladies' Nights

Stretch your drinking budget by taking advantage of happy hour deals, which are offered by all types of bars from dives to five-star glamour pits. Many also go to extraordinary lengths to lure the 'fairer gender' with free cocktails, bubbly and nibbles during ladies' nights, especially on Tuesdays.

Sheesha & Mocktails

Most Emiratis don't drink alcohol and prefer to socialise around coffee, juices and mocktails. Join them in a mellow *sheesha* cafe and sample a puff to better understand this Middle Eastern pastime practiced by both men and women. Most places also serve elaborate mocktails.

☑ Top Tips

▶ Dubai has zero-tolerance laws on drink driving. Getting caught could entail fines or jail time. Even being drunk in public may subject you to prosecution.

▶ Bars and pubs also serve food.

Best Beachfront Bars

360° Sizzling offshore party perch for watching the sun drop behind the Burj Al Arab. (p78)

Jetty Lounge Sip artful potions at this classy and sensuously styled bar. (p116)

Bliss Lounge Chilled Dubai Marina dispensary of top cocktails. (p117)

View from 360° bar with the Burj Al Arab in the background

Best Rooftop Bars

Siddharta Cocktails with Dubai Marina views at this ab-fab lounge by the pool. (p117)

Dek on 8 An unpretentious vibe draws creatives for cocktails and weekend parties. (p117)

Atelier M Stylish entry with stellar perch atop the Pier 7 building in the Marina. (p116)

Best Happy Hour & Ladies' Nights

Calabar Kickstart the night with half-price drinks daily from 6pm to 8pm at this sleek Downtown alfresco lounge. (p98)

Pure Sky Lounge Sunsets over the Gulf go well with 50% off drinks daily between 5pm and 7pm. (p118)

Barasti Beachfront institution with daily deals between 4pm and 7pm, plus Dh50 free-flowing sparkly on Ladies' Tuesdays. (p116)

Best Pubs

Irish Village A congenial Irish pub with blarney decor, a leafy setting and regular live music. (p34)

George & Dragon Channel your inner Bukowski at this hard-core barfly hangout. (p53)

Best for Sheesha & Mocktails

Kan Zaman Count the colours of the Creek while puffing away at this waterfront lounge. (p50)

Mazology Hipsters get high on high-octane sounds and romantic Gulf views at this beachfront hangout. (p79)

Kris Kros Urban outpost with Burj Khalifa views and an encyclopaedia of booze-free drinks and *sheesha*. (p97)

Best Bars with a View

Bahri Bar Romantic space overlooking the Madinat Jumeirah canals and Burj Al Arab. (p79)

Neos High-in-the-sky bar with art deco flourishes and killer cocktails. (p97)

QDs Chill outdoor lounge overlooking the Creek. (p34)

DARYL VISSCHER / CORBIS ©

Best
Shopping

Shopping is a favourite pastime in Dubai, home to the world's largest mall and shopping centres that look like ancient Egypt or an Italian village and feature ski slopes, ice rinks and giant aquariums. Souqs provide more traditional flair, and a growing crop of outdoor malls, indie boutiques and galleries beckon as well.

Trends

A recent fad has seen the arrival of the outdoor mall. Places such as the Beach at JBR in the Dubai Marina or the City Walk in Downtown Dubai feature a smaller selection of stores calibrated to the needs and tastes of local residents. There's also a growing number of indie designer boutiques, especially along Jumeirah Rd.

Bargaining Basics

Prices are fixed in malls and most stores, but in souqs and outdoor markets it pays to know some bargaining basics. A good rule of thumb is to cut the first suggested price in half and go from there. Expect to finish up with a discount of 20% to 30%. If you intend to buy more than one item, use this as a bargaining chip. For more, see p56.

Bedouin Jewellery

Bedouin jewellery is a brilliant buy and, given the steady boho-chic trend, makes a great gift. Look for elaborate silver necklaces and pendants, chunky earrings and rings, and wedding belts, many of which incorporate turquoise and semi-precious stones. Very little of the older Bedouin jewellery comes from the Emirates; most of it originates in Oman, Yemen and Afghanistan. Cheaper stuff usually hails from India.

☑ **Top Tips**

▶ Buy fragrant Iranian and Spanish saffron at reasonable prices.

▶ Try before you buy and ask about return policies, especially for gifts.

▶ Most major malls are open from 10am to 10pm (to 11pm or midnight on Thursday and Friday).

Best Shopping Malls

Dubai Mall A power shopper's Shangri-La, this is the largest mall in the world (and still growing). (p99)

Mall of the Emirates Get lost amid the ample temptations of the

AMANDA HALL / GETTY IMAGES ©

Dubai Mall interior

mega-mall famous for its indoor ski slope. (p80)

Deira City Centre A no-nonsense shopping mall with a satisfying mix of international chains and indie stores. (p35)

Best for Fashion

West LA Boutique The holy grail for fashionistas wanting to dress like young Hollywood royalty. (p80)

O-Concept This edgy Jumeirah boutique has young things looking good at reasonable price tags. (p64)

O' de Rose Provides a platform for regional indie designers with a love for bold colour. (p81)

S*uce Growing Emirati emporium of sassy avant-garde fashions from young international designers. (p64)

Best for Gifts

Camel Company Go camel-crazy at this boutique starring cuddly dromedaries. (p81)

Bateel Delicious dates presented like precious jewels in an elegant boutique setting. (p55)

Ajmal Exotic Arabian essential oils and perfumes sold in exquisitely beautiful bottles. (p57)

Tehran Persian Carpets & Antiques A mind-boggling bonanza of quality souvenirs from Iran, surpassing its namesake products. (p100)

Yasmine Fabulous assortment of quality pashminas, including precious hand-embroidered ones. (p80)

Best Modern Souqs

Souk Al Bahar Across from Dubai Mall, this richly decorated Arabesque souq teems with restaurants and souvenir stores. (p90)

Souk Madinat Jumeirah Following a harmonious rhythm of courtyards, alleyways and outdoor areas, this souq also has a theatre and lots of cafes and restaurants fronting the Madinat canals. (p68)

Best
Beaches

Dubai's locals love their beaches. Jumeirah and Dubai Marina residents who live within splashing distance of the crystal-clear turquoise waters make it a daily ritual to head down to the beach, while the rest of Dubai typically hits the sand on Fridays and Saturdays. Beach parks are also popular, as much for family barbecues as for swimming and sunbathing.

KAMI KAMI / GETTY IMAGES ©

Facilities & Activities

If you're not staying at a beachfront hotel fronted by its own sandy ribbon, you can either drop big dirham for a day guest pass, pay to chill at a snazzy beach club or go dipping for free at a public beach. The latter are clean and come with changing rooms, toilets, playgrounds, barbecue pits and kiosks. The 14km-long Jumeirah Corniche, which opened in late 2014, parallels the Gulf from the Dubai Marine Beach Resort to the Burj Al Arab and features a boardwalk, a bouncy jogging track, kiosks and benches. Some sections, though, are actually closed for the foreseeable future,

most notably Jumeirah Beach Park and Jumeirah Open Beach.

Best Free Beaches

Kite Beach Glorious stretch of sand for active types with kite surfing, volleyball, soap football and other fun and games. (p76)

JBR Open Beach This long Dubai Marina strip is flanked by showers, children's fun zones and plenty of restaurants. (p108)

Sunset Beach Overlooking the Burj Al Arab, this is the beach where you shouldn't forget your camera. (p71)

Al Mamzar Beach Park Huge, pristine and family-friendly with a pool, playgrounds and

water sports but few food outlets. (p29)

Best Beach Clubs

Club Mina A big hit with families thanks to five pools and a 500m-long sweep of pristine beach. (p110)

Zero Gravity Chilled but chic bar-restaurant-club combo right next to the Drop Zone of Skydive Dubai. (p109)

Meydan Beach Club A sexy, grown-up vibe rules this posh outpost with a spa and infinity pool. (p110)

25' Beach Club On Palm Jumeirah, this low-key club is popular with families and has nice views back to the mainland skyline. (p110)

Best
Art

Fuelled by artists from around the world, Dubai's art scene has become one of the most dynamic in the Gulf region. Although there are no public art museums, art aficionados will find their compass on perpetual spin with a growing number of galleries, private collections, officially sanctioned street art, several high-profile art events and fairs.

COURTESY ALSERKAL AVENUE, DUBAI

☑ **Top Tip**

▶ Most galleries are closed from Friday to Saturday afternoon.

Gallery Quarters

Galleries in Dubai cluster in two main areas. Emerging, underground and experimental art has found a home in the gritty streets of industrial Al Quoz with the Alserkal Avenue campus as its centrepiece. More established contenders have decamped to Gate Village, an adjunct to the Dubai International Finance Center. Dubai art world pioneers can be found in Bur Dubai's Al Fahidi Historic District.

Dubai Art Week

Collectors, dealers, curators, artists, gallery owners and art fans mark their calendars for Dubai Art Week, held annually in March since 2007. It centres on **Art Dubai** (www.artdubai.ae), a prestigious gathering of nearly 100 galleries from the UAE and around the world at Madinat Jumeirah. It is accompanied by Design Days Dubai and the **Sikka Art Fair** (www.sikka.ae), which sees around 50 local artists create site-specific works in the Al Fahidi Historic District.

Best for Middle Eastern Art

Ayyam Gallery This top international gallery has branches in both Al Quoz and Gate Village. (p90)

Third Line Represents top regional artists here and at international art fairs. (p73)

XVA Gallery Art-world top dogs and promising up-and-comers in a heritage building. (p46)

Gallery Isabelle van den Eynde Shepherds regional emerging and midcareer artists to prominence. (p73)

Best for International Art

Empty Quarter Dedicated to photography. (p90)

Majlis Gallery Dubai gallery pioneer presents paintings, ceramics and glass art. (p43)

Best
Architecture

The juxtaposition of traditional Arabian architecture and futuristic structures is a metaphor for what makes Dubai tick. Although some recent developments, such as Madinat Jumeirah, have seen a return to traditional Arabian forms, headline-grabbing projects such as the Burj Khalifa show that the cloud-busting skyscraper isn't going anywhere in Dubai but up.

RAGA JOSE FUSTE / ROBERT HARDING ©

Traditional Emirati Buildings

The Al Ras neighbourhood in northern Deira and the Shindagha and Al Fahidi historic districts in Bur Dubai are great places to see and enter traditional Emirati buildings. Made from gypsum and coral, they typically wrap around a central courtyard flanked by verandahs to keep direct sunlight out of the rooms. Another distinctive feature are the *barjeel* (wind towers), a form of nonelectrical air-conditioning unique to the region. Open on all four sides, they can catch even the tiniest of breezes, which are then channelled down a central shaft and into the room below.

Best Heritage Architecture

Shindagha Historic District Previous generations of Dubai rulers made their homes in these restored Creek-facing residences-turned-museums. (p46)

Al Fahidi Historic District A wander around this restored quarter is an eye-opening journey into Dubai's past. (p42)

Al Ahmadiya School Dubai's first school was founded by the pearl merchant who once lived in the adjacent Heritage House. (p28)

☑ **Top Tip**

▶ Book ahead to visit the Burj Khalifa or the Burj Al Arab.

Dubai Museum A survey of Dubai's history within the confines of the Al Fahidi Fort, Dubai's oldest building. (p40)

Best Iconic Buildings

Burj Al Arab This 60-floor, sail-shaped hotel is 321m high and sits on its own artificial island linked to the mainland by a causeway. (p70)

Burj Khalifa The design of the world's tallest building (828m) was inspired by a desert flower. (p86)

Best
Sporting Events

Best Events

Dubai World Cup (www.dubaiworldcup.com) Dubai's horse racing season culminates in March with the world's richest event (a record-holding US$10 million purse) held at the Meydan Racecourse. While there's no betting, this is the city's biggest social event.

Dubai Tennis Championships (www.dubaidutyfreetennischampionships.com) Top-ranked players volley away at this two-week pro event in February. It's a great opportunity to see some great hitting in the relatively small Aviation Stadium.

Dubai Desert Classic (www.dubaidesertclassic.com) The golfing elite comes to town for this February tournament known for its thrilling finishes – the 18th hole has become legendary on the PGA circuit.

Dubai Marathon (www.dubaimarathon.org) Sweat it out in January with thousands of other runners or just cheer during this popular street race with a prize fund of $1 million. Less-energetic types can enter a 10km run or a 3km 'fun run'.

Dubai Rugby Sevens (www.dubairugby7s.com) Held in November or December, the first round of the eight-leg International Rugby Board Sevens World Series attracts up to 150,000 spectators. The stadium is about 30 minutes south of Dubai on the road to Al Ain.

Camel Racing Season Runs from October to early April. The closest track to Dubai is Al Marmoun, about 40km south of town en route to Al Ain. Check www.dubaicalendar.ae (search for 'camel') for the schedule.

DP World Tour Championship (www.europeantour.com) This November golf championship is the crowning tournament of the Race to Dubai that pits the PGA European Tour's top players

☑ **Top Tip**

▶ Book tickets far in advance via either the event website or online agencies such as www.platinumlist.net.

against each other. Held since 2008, it comes with a purse of US$7.5 million. It's played on two Greg Norman–designed courses at Jumeirah Golf Estates.

Abu Dhabi Grand Prix (www.senategrandprix-abu-dhabi.com) Every year the Formula 1 racing elite, including Sebastian Vettel and Lewis Hamilton, descends upon the wicked 5.5km-long Yas Marina Circuit on Abu Dhabi's Yas Island in early November.

Best
For Kids

JOHN BORTHWICK / GETTY IMAGES

Travelling to Dubai with kids can be child's play, especially if you keep a light schedule and involve them in day-to-day planning. There's plenty to do from water parks and playgrounds to theme parks and activity centres. Most beach hotels operate kids clubs, letting you work on your tan or kip off to the spa.

Junior Foodies

It's perfectly fine to bring your kids to all but the most formal restaurants, although they (and you) might feel more relaxed at casual cafes, bistros and family restaurants. Malls boast extensive food courts where kids can browse and pick what they like. Hotels have at least one restaurant suitable for families, usually the 24-hour cafe or the buffet restaurant.

Playgrounds & Parks

Though you won't want to visit them during the sunburn season of July and August, Dubai has a handful of parks with picnic areas and playgrounds for children to let off steam. One of the biggest and best for activities is Za'abeel Park, with great sports facilities, a viewing tower and a lake.

Teen Time

OK, so they've done the ski slopes, disco-danced at the ice rink, splashed around at the water parks and enjoyed a fashionable strut around the malls. Is there more to prevent teens from succumbing to boredom? For the ultimate holiday pic to impress their pals back home, consider taking them sandboarding, camel riding on an overnight desert safari or even a trekking trip to the Hajar Mountains. Tours are offered by numerous companies, including Arabian Adventures.

☑ Top Tips

► For general advice, see Lonely Planet's *Travel with Children*.

► For babysitting, ask for a referral at your hotel or try www.dubaimetro maids.com or www. maidszone.com.

► Children under five travel free on public transport.

Best Water Parks

Aquaventure One of the largest water parks in the world with rides suitable for the entire family. (p109)

Wild Wadi Waterpark The original family-favourite, catering to

Visitors at Dubai Aquarium, Dubai Mall (p85)

every age with attractions ranging from gentle pools to kamikaze slides. (p76)

Best Themed Attractions

KidZania Built around an interactive miniature city, this attraction offers the ultimate in role-play options. (p91)

Sega Republic Older kids can get their kicks at this indoor game park with fairly tame thrill rides, arcade games and motion-simulators. (p92)

Best for Animal Attractions

Dubai Aquarium & Underwater Zoo Kids will be mesmerised by the sharks, groupers and rays flitting about this giant three-story aquarium in Dubai Mall. (p85)

Lost Chambers For another audience with fishy friends, head to this labyrinth of underwater tanks and tunnels teeming with exotic denizens at Atlantis The Palm. (p108)

Dubai Dino This bony buddy was born in Wyoming 155 million years ago and moved to Dubai Mall in 2014. (p85)

Best for Chilled-Out Kids

Dubai Ice Rink Tots to teens can cool down with pirouettes and disco dancing at Dubai Mall's ice rink. (p91)

Ski Dubai Alpine slopes, toboggan tracks and penguin encounters await at this massive indoor winter wonderland. (p76)

Best
Clubbing

DJs spin every night of the week with the top names hitting the decks on Thursdays and Fridays. Partying is not restricted to the evening, with plenty of beach clubs kicking into gear in the early afternoon on weekends in the cooler months. The sound repertoire is global – funk, soul, trip-hop, hip hop, R&B, African, Arabic and Latino – although the emphasis is still clearly on house and EDM (electronic dance music).

JONATHAN AYLIFFE / GETTY IMAGES ©

Global DJs

Globetrotting big-name DJs such as Ellen Allien, Carl Craig, Ricardo Villalobos and Roger Sanchez occasionally jet in for the weekend to whip the crowd into a frenzy at top venues and megaparties such as Groove on the Grass or White Dubai. Homegrown talent to keep on the radar include DJs Raxon, Danny Neville, Shadow and Beatz.

Parties

Some of the best club nights are weekly or monthly residencies put on by local promoters in top clubs around town. Major draws include the Friday 'Sunset Sessions' hosted by local record label Audio Tonic at 360°; Jamrock Dubai (varous venues), which introduced reggae, soca and dancehall artists to the region; and Electric Night, currently at Tamanya Terrace.

At the Door

Doors are tough at many clubs. Check a venue's website or Facebook page for a possible dress code. Generally speaking, beachside venues are more relaxed and underground clubs tend not to have a door policy at all. All-men groups have little chance of getting in anywhere, though.

☑ **Top Tip**

▶ Keep tabs on the latest club world happenings with the free *Hype* magazine, available at hip bars, boutiques and spas around town, and digitally via the iTunes app store and **Magzter** (www. magzter.com).

▶ Other listings: www.residentadvisor. net, www.infusion.ae, www.platinumlist.ae, www.timeoutdubai. com.

▶ Clubs open around 9pm, get going around 11pm and close at 3am.

DARYL VISSCHER / GETTY IMAGES ©

Outdoor partying at 360° bar

Best for Top DJs

Pacha Ibiza Dubai The Balearic island legend has imported its hot-stepping action to Dubai. (p79)

N'Dulge Megaclub at the Atlantis brings inter-national DJs behind the turntables. (p119)

Best for Outdoor Partying

Nasimi Beach Cool beats combine with glittering skyline views and a cosmopolitan vibe at Atlantis The Palm. (p118)

Zero Gravity Go from chill to charged at this day-to-night club with at-tached beach, lounge and restaurant. (p109)

Barasti Any time is a good time to stumble into the original party village in the sand. (p116)

360° Watch the sun drop behind the Burj Al Arab at this sizzling offshore party den. (p78)

Best for Underground Vibe

Basement Plug into the local DJ scene while keeping it real with an eclectic sound range. (p116)

Dek on 8 Unpretentious vibe draws media types for cocktails and week-end parties. (p117)

Music Room Top place for plugging into the local live music scene. (p54)

Best Glam Factor

The Act Newcomer shakes things up with cabaret acts amid Vic-torian theatre lushness. (p97)

Boudoir Swish venue for beautiful people gyrating to a sound mix from hip-hop to *desi* (Bollywood). (p64)

People by Crystal Be dazzled by the decor and crowd on the top two floors of the pyramid-shaped Raffles. (p53)

Cavalli Club Bling brig-aders should strap on those heels and make a beeline to this sparkling dancing den. (p98)

Best
Tours

If you're a Dubai first-timer, letting someone else show you around is a fun and efficient way to get your bearings, see the key sights quickly and obtain a general understanding of the city. All manner of exploration – from city bus tours to mosque visits – is available.

Dubai In-Depth

Dubai offers a growing number of guided explorations to match all sorts of interests. Take a classic bus tour if you just want to get an introduction to the city or join a themed walking tour for an in-depth look at certain facets of daily life. Based in Bur Dubai, the nonprofit **Sheikh Mohammed Centre for Cultural Understanding** (p48) offers the best cultural tours to introduce visitors to facets of Emirati culture, including traditions, customs and religion. They're the only ones who take non-Muslims inside a mosque and also offer breakfasts and lunches where you can taste the local cuisine. Hard-core foodies, though, should sign on with Arva Arved's Frying Pan Adventures for a mouthwatering immersion in Dubai street food culture.

Best Walking Tours

Al Fahidi Historic District Peel back the curtain on Dubai's distant past on a tour with the Sheikh Mohammed Centre for Cultural Understanding. (p48)

Frying Pan Adventures Plunge headlong into the culinary labyrinth of multicultural Bur Dubai and Deira on these fun and educational guided food tours. (p50)

Jumeirah Mosque The only mosque in Dubai that can be visited by non-Muslims; guided tours offered daily except Friday. (p62)

Best Bus Tours

Big Bus Dubai Hop-on, hop-off tours with taped commentary in 12 languages link all of Dubai's major sights and landmarks on three interconnecting routes. (p49)

Wonder Bus Discover Dubai's historic centre on one-hour land and water tours aboard an ingenious amphibious bus. (p49)

Best Boat Tours

Dubai Ferry Value-priced minicruises let you appreciate the city skyline from the water. (p111)

Al Mansour Dhow Float past the glittering Creek lights while indulging in a buffet dinner on a historic dhow. (p32)

Survival Guide

Survival Guide

Before You Go

When to Go

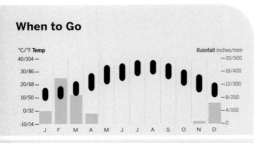

°C/°F Temp
40/104 —
30/86 —
20/68 —
10/50 —
0/32 —
-10/14 —

Rainfall inches/mm
— 20/500
— 16/400
— 12/300
— 8/200
— 4/100
— 0

J F M A M J J A S O N D

➡ **Winter (Dec–Feb)**
Moderate temperatures, short days, occasional rain, many festivals and activities.

➡ **Spring (Mar–Apr)**
Perfect beach weather with temperatures around 30°C.

➡ **Summer (Jul–Sep)**
Temperatures soar (to an average 43°C with stifling 95% humidity), hotel rates drop.

➡ **Autumn (Oct–Nov)**
Warm weather, balmy nights, life moves back outdoors.

Book Your Stay

☑ **Top Tip** Most properties have an internet booking function with a best-price guarantee.

➡ A 10% room tax, 10% service fee and a 'tourism tax' ranging from Dh7 to Dh20 per night are added to room rates.

➡ Even midrange hotels often have superb facilities, including a pool, multiple restaurants, a gym, satellite TV and a bar.

➡ Not all hotels are licensed to serve alcohol, so check if this is important to you.

➡ Hotel apartments are great for self-caterers, families and groups.

➡ Nostalgic types should check into the growing crop of heritage boutique hotels in Bur Dubai and Deira.

➡ By law, unmarried men and women are not permitted to share a room, but in reality most hotels turn a blind eye.

➡ Free wi-fi is common-place but access may be weak in some rooms or restricted to public areas.

➡ Room rates fluctuate enormously, spiking during festivals, holidays and big events and plummeting in summer.

Useful Websites

Lonely Planet (www.lonelyplanet.com/hotels) Lonely Planet's online booking service, with the lowdown on the best places to stay.

Dubai Tourism (www.dubaitourism.ae) The site run by Dubai's official tourist authority also has a booking function.

Dubai Apartments (www.dubaiapartments.biz) Private booking site specialised in hotel apartments.

Best Budget

Barjeel Heritage Guest House (www.barjeelguesthouse.com) Dream sweetly at this historic Bur Dubai Creekside charmer straight out of *Arabian Nights*.

Grand Midwest Tower (www.gmwhotels.com) Steps from a metro station and close to Dubai Marina,

this city hotel offers four-star comforts, often at two-star rates.

Four Points by Sheraton Bur Dubai (www.fourpointsburdubai.com) Top-value chain in great location with a small pool and two excellent restaurants.

Coral Dubai Deira Hotel (www.hmhhotelgroup.com) Close to great budget eats and the airport, the Coral hides considerable comforts behind its business demeanour.

Ibis World Trade Centre (www.ibis.com) Dependable low-frills chain hotel with

generous public areas but pocket-sized rooms.

Best Midrange

Centro Barsha (www.rotana.com/centrobarsha) An excellent value-for-money pick near Mall of the Emirates.

Beach Hotel Apartment (http://beachhotelapartment.ae) A rare bargain in Jumeirah with easy access to beaches and shopping.

Media One Hotel (www.mediaonehotel.com) High-octane Dubai Media City hot spot with mod design and party pedigree.

Dos & Don'ts

➡ Do ask before taking a photo of locals.

➡ Do remove your shoes before entering an Emirati home.

➡ Do accept any hospitality offered; for example, coffee or dates.

➡ Do dress modestly outside the perimeters of your hotel or resort.

➡ Do wear swimwear at the beach, but no thongs.

➡ Don't swear, shout or make offensive gestures (giving the finger, sticking out your tongue etc).

➡ Don't get drunk in public places as it may lead to fines or possibly jail time.

➡ Don't point your finger or the soles of your feet towards locals.

➡ Don't indulge in public displays of affection (holding hands is OK).

Pearl Marina Hotel Apartments (www.pearl marinahotel.com) All of the charms of Dubai Marina at your feet without having to rob a bank.

XVA Hotel (www.xvahotel. com) Connect to the magic of yesteryear in this art-filled heritage den in Bur Dubai.

Best Top End

One&Only Royal Mirage (http://royalmirage.oneand onlyresorts.com) Sumptuous and sprawling beach resort with palatial Arabian-style architecture and expansive gardens.

Palace Downtown Dubai (www.theaddress.com) Romantic downtown pad with easy access to top shopping and Instagram-worthy views of Burj Khalifa.

Grosvenor House (www. grosvenorhouse-dubai.com) Dubai Marina option draws local cognoscenti to its hip bars and restaurants.

Park Hyatt Dubai (www. dubai.park.hyatt.com) A class act in Deira surrounded by lush landscaping with superb facilities and golf course access.

Mina A' Salam (www. jumeirah.com) A warm

Madinat Jumeirah beachfront port of call for blue-sky holiday cravers.

Arriving in Dubai

☑ For the best way to get to your accommodation, see p17.

Dubai International Airport

➡ Dubai metro runs from 5.30am to midnight (2am Thursday and Friday) from terminals 1 and 3.

➡ Getting caught with alcohol on the metro (even if purchased at the airport duty-free shop) entails a Dh500 fine.

➡ A maximum of one medium-size and one small piece of luggage are allowed on the trains.

➡ Airport taxis have a starting meter of Dh25 and a per-kilometre charge of Dh1.86.

➡ Approximate taxi fares are Dh45 to Deira or Bur Dubai, Dh60 to Downtown Dubai, Dh80 to Madinat Jumeirah and Dh90 to Dubai Marina.

Getting Around

Metro
☑ **Best for...** price and speed.

➡ Dubai metro operates on two lines. The Red Line links Rashidiya near Dubai International Airport with Jebel Ali past Dubai Marina, handily paralleling Sheikh Zayed Rd. The Green Line links Etisalat, northwest of the airport, with Creek Park.

➡ Trains run roughly every 10 minutes from 5.30am to midnight (to 2am Thursday and Friday).

➡ Each train consists of five cars. The front car is divided into a women-only section and a 'gold class' section where a double fare buys leather seating and carpeted floors.

➡ For details and trip planning, visit www.rta.ae.

Taxi
☑ **Best for...** convenience.

➡ Dubai has a large, modern fleet of metered taxis. Expect long waits during peak hours and at shopping malls.

➡ The starting fare for nonairport taxis is Dh5, plus Dh1.71 per kilometre; tolls are included, tips are not (round up to the nearest note).

➡ Taxis can be flagged down or picked up at ranks.

➡ Rather than asking to be taken to a specific street address, specify the nearest landmark (eg a hotel, mall, roundabout). If your cabbie is lost, ask him to radio his office for directions.

➡ For details, including a taxi fare calculator, see www.dubaitaxi.ae.

Boat
☑ **Best for...** scenic rides.

➡ *Abras* (traditional wooden boats; Dh1) are a wonderful way to cross the Creek.

➡ Water buses (Dh2 to 5 per trip) are air-conditioned and operate at the Dubai Marina and along Dubai Creek.

➡ Dubai Ferry runs sightseeing trips from Dubai Marina and the Creek (Dh50).

Nol Cards

➡ Before hopping on a bus, water bus or metro train you must purchase a rechargeable Nol card from ticket offices or vending machines at metro stations and many bus stations.

➡ Short-term visitors should get the Red Card, which costs Dh2 and may be topped up with up to 10 journeys. Trips cost between Dh4 and Dh8.50.

➡ If you intend to make more than 10 trips, get a Silver Card for Dh25 (including Dh19 of credit). Trips are charged at Dh3 to Dh7.50. The Gold Card costs the same but trips are charged at double the price for access to the gold-class carriage.

➡ The correct fare is automatically deducted when swiping your card upon entering and exiting public transport.

➡ Children under age five travel free.

➡ For full details, see www.nol.ae.

Bus
☑ **Best for...** local travel.

➡ Buses are clean, comfortable and air-conditioned but slow. The front section is reserved for women and families.

➡ Most routes operate at 15- to 20-minute intervals between 6am and 11.30pm (later and less frequently on Fridays). On some routes night buses take over at 30-minute intervals in the interim.

➡ For details and trip planning, visit www.dubai-bus.com or www.rta.ae.

Essential Information

Business Hours
☑ **Top Tip** Opening hours are curtailed during Ramadan.

Restaurants Noon to 3pm and 7.30pm to midnight.

Shopping malls 10am to 10pm Saturday to Wednesday, to midnight Thursday and Friday.

Souqs 9am to 1pm and 4pm to 9pm Saturday to Thursday, 4pm to 9pm Friday.

Electricity

220V/50Hz

Emergencies
Ambulance (☏ 999)
Fire Department (☏ 997)
Police (☏ 999)

Money
☑ **Top Tip** Bring cash and bargaining acumen to the souqs as credit cards are not widely accepted.

➡ The UAE dirham (Dh) is pegged to the US dollar. One dirham is divided into 100 fils.

➡ Globally linked ATMs can be found all over the city. Check with your bank about possible fees and charges.

➡ Exchange offices tend to offer better rates than banks. Reliable outlets include UAE Exchange or Al Rostamani, both with multiple branches in shopping malls and around town.

➡ Major credit cards are widely accepted; debit cards less so, although they're usually fine at bigger retail outlets.

Public Holidays
☑ **Top Tip** During Ramadan, bar hours are restricted and clubs closed altogether.

Hejira Islamic New Year

Eid al-Fitr Three-day celebration that ends Ramadan fasting.

Eid al-Adha Four-day celebration following

Money-Saving Tips
➡ Museums are either free or charge just a few dirham for admission.

➡ Top attractions such as the Dubai Fountains, the souqs and the Creek waterfront are also free.

➡ Take advantage of deals on drinks and nibbles during happy hours and ladies' nights.

➡ Travel on the Dubai metro for longer distances and only use a taxi to get to your final destination.

➡ Fuel up for pocket change on curries, kebabs, shwarma, samosas, dosas, momos and other exotic and delicious delectables brought to Dubai by its global expats.

➡ Check out top thoroughbreds or gangly dromedaries at highly popular horse and camel races – admission is free.

➡ If you can stand the heat, visit in July or August when hotel prices plummet.

Islamic Holidays

ISLAMIC YEAR	HEJIRA	PROPHET'S BIRTHDAY	RAMADAN	EID AL-FITR	EID AL-ADHA
1436 (2015)	25 Oct	24 Dec	18 Jun	17 Jul	23 Sep
1437 (2016)	3 Oct	12 Dec	7 Jun	7 Jul	13 Sep
1438 (2017)	22 Sep	1 Dec	27 May	26 Jun	2 Sep

the main pilgrimage to Mecca, the hajj.

Ramadan The month when Muslims fast during daylight hours.

Prophet's Birthday One-day holiday for the public sector.

Safe Travel

There is zero tolerance for drug possession and use and getting caught is severely punished with fines, jail time and deportation. The import of certain prescription medicines is also restricted unless you can present a prescription (preferably accompanied by a letter) issued by a licensed doctor to prove that you need them. For a list, see www.uaeinteract.com/travel/drug.asp.

If you have an accident, even a small one, you must call the police (☞999) and wait at the scene. If it's a minor accident, move your car to the side of the road. You cannot file an insurance claim without a police report.

Dubai is a safe city for women and it's fine to take cabs and walk around on your own. Modest dress is recommended but there's no need to cover up.

Telephone

☑ **Top Tip** Skype is still blocked in the UAE, but many people get around this by downloading a proxy bypass or VPN.

➡ Local landline-to-landline calls are free within the same emirate.

➡ To phone another country from the UAE, dial ☞00 followed by the country code.

➡ To call the UAE, dial the country code ☞971.

Mobile Phones

The UAE's mobile-phone network uses the GSM 900 MHz and 1800 MHz standard. If you don't have a worldwide roaming service but do have an unlocked phone, consider buying a prepaid SIM card from local providers Etisalat or Du, available at the airport, telecom stores and convenience stores. 3G and 4G are available.

Tourist Information

Dubai Tourism & Commerce Marketing (www.dubaitourism.ae) operates two 24-hour kiosks in terminals 1 and 3 of the Dubai International Airport.

Visas

At the time of writing, citizens of 45 countries get free on-the-spot 30-day tourist visas upon arrival in the UAE. Everyone else must have a visa arranged through a sponsor, such as your UAE hotel or tour operator, prior to arrival.

Entry requirements can change at the drop of a hat, so always confirm the latest regulations with a UAE consulate in your home country.

Language

MSA (Modern Standard Arabic) –
the official lingua franca of the Arab
world – and the everyday spoken
version are quite different. The Arabic
variety spoken in Dubai (and provided
in this chapter) is known as Gulf Arabic.

Note that *gh* is a throaty sound
(like the French 'r'), *r* is rolled, *dh* is
pronounced as the 'th' in 'that', *th* as in
'thin', *ch* as in 'cheat' and *kh* as the 'ch'
in the Scottish *loch*. The apostrophe
(') indicates the glottal stop (like the
pause in the middle of 'uh-oh'). Bearing
these few points in mind and reading
our pronunciation guides as if they
were English, you'll be understood.
The stressed syllables are indicated
with italics. The markers (m) and (f)
indicate masculine and feminine word
forms respectively.

To enhance your trip with a phrase-
book, visit **lonelyplanet.com**. Lonely
Planet iPhone phrasebooks are available through the Apple App store.

Basics

Hello.
اهلا و سهلا. *ah*·lan was *ah*·lan

Goodbye.
مع السلامة. ma' sa·*laa*·ma

Yes./No.
نعم./لا. *na*·am/la

Please.
من فضلك. min *fad*·lak (m)
من فضلك. min *fad*·lik (f)

Thank you.
شكران. *shuk*·ran

Excuse me.
اسمح لي. is·*mah* lee (m)
اسمحي لي. is·mah·ee lee (f)

Sorry.
مع الاسف. ma'·al·*as*·af

Do you speak English?
تتكلم/تتكلمي tit·*kal*·am/tit·*ka*·la·mee
انجليزية؟ in·glee·*zee*·ya (m/f)

I don't understand.
مو فاهم. moo *faa*·him

Eating & Drinking

I'd like (the) ..., please.
عطني/عطيني 'a·ti·nee/'a·*tee*·nee
الـ ... من فضلك. il ... min *fad*·lak (m/f)

bill	قائمة	*kaa*·'i·ma
drink list	قائمة	*kaa*·'i·mat
	المشروبات	il·mash·roo·*baat*
menu	الطعام	*kaa*·'i·mat
	قائمة	i·ta·*aam*
that dish	الطبق	i·*tab*·ak
	هاذاك	haa·*dhaa*·ka

What would you recommend?
اش تنصح؟ aash *tan*·sah (m)
اش تنصحي؟ aash *tan*·sa·hee (f)

Do you have vegetarian food?
عندك طعم 'an·dak ta·*'am*
نباتي؟ na·*baa*·tee

Shopping

I'm looking for ...
مدور على ... moo·*daw*·ir 'a·la ... (m)
مدورة على ... moo·*daw*·i·ra 'a·la ... (f)

Can I look at it?
ممكن اشوف؟ *mum*·kin a·*shoof*

How much is it?
بكم؟ bi·*kam*

That's too expensive.
غالي جداً.   *ghaa·lee jid·*an

What's your lowest price?
اش السعر الاخر؟   aash i·*si'r* il·*aa·*khir

Do you have any others?
عندك اخرين؟   *'and·*ak ukh·*reen* (m)
عندك اخرين؟   *'and·*ik ukh·*reen* (f)

Emergencies

Help!
مساعد!   moo·*saa·*'id (m)
مساعدة!   moo·*saa·*'id·a (f)

Call a doctor!
تصل/تصلي   ti·sil/ti·si·lee
على طبيب!   *'a·*la ta·*beeb* (m/f)

Call the police!
تصل/تصلي   ti·sil/ti·si·lee
على الشرطة!   *'a·*la i·*shur·*ta (m/f)

I'm lost.
انا ضعت.   *a·*na duht

I'm sick.
انا مريض.   *a·*na ma·*reed* (m)
انا مريضة.   *a·*na ma·*ree·*da (f)

Where are the toilets?
وين المرحاض؟   wayn il·mir·*haad*

Time & Numbers

What time is it?/At what time?
الساعة كم؟   i·*saa·*a' kam

It's/At (two) o'clock.
الساعة (ثنتين).   i·*saa·*a' (thin·*tayn*)

yesterday ...   البارح ...   il·*baa·*rih ...

tomorrow ...   باكر ...   *baa·*chir ...

  morning   صباح   sa·*baah*
  afternoon   بعد الظهر   ba'd a·*thuhr*
  evening   مساء   *mi·saa*

1	١	واحد	*waa·*hid
2	٢	اثنين	ith·*nayn*
3	٣	ثلاثة	tha·*laa·*tha
4	٤	اربع	ar·*ba'*
5	٥	خمسة	*kham·*sa
6	٦	ستة	*si·*ta
7	٧	سبعة	*sa·*ba'
8	٨	ثمانية	tha·*maan·*ya
9	٩	تسعة	*tis·*a'
10	١٠	عشرة	*'ash·*ar·a
100	١٠٠	مية	*mee·*ya
1000	١٠٠٠	الف	alf

Transport & Directions

Where's the ...?
من وين ...؟   min wayn ...

What's the address?
ما العنوان؟   ma il·'un·*waan*

Can you show me (on the map)?
لو سمحت   law sa·*maht*
وريني   wa·*ree·*nee
(علخريطة)؟   ('al·kha·*ree·*ta)

How far is it?
كم بعيد؟   kam ba·*'eed*

Please take me to (this address).
من فضلك خذني   min *fad·*lak *khudh·*nee
(علعنوان هاذا).   ('al·'un·*waan* haa·dha)

Please stop here.
لو سمحت   law sa·*maht*
وقف هنا.   wa·*gif* hi·na

What time's the bus?
الساعة كم   a·*saa·*a' kam
الباص؟   il·*baas*

What station/stop is this?
ما هي   maa *hee·*ya
المحطة هاذي؟   il·ma·ha·ta haa·dhee

Behind the Scenes

Send Us Your Feedback

We love to hear from travellers – your comments help make our books better. We read every word, and we guarantee that your feedback goes straight to the authors. Visit **lonelyplanet.com/contact** to submit your updates and suggestions.

Note: We may edit, reproduce and incorporate your comments in Lonely Planet products such as guidebooks, websites and digital products, so let us know if you don't want your comments reproduced or your name acknowledged. For a copy of our privacy policy visit lonelyplanet.com/privacy.

Andrea's Thanks

Big thanks to the many wonderful people who plied me with tips, insights and ideas and/or opened doors throughout Dubai, including Katie King, Caitriona Gaffney, Sandra Farrero, Sarah Hameister, Melanie Dautry, Nivine William, Sarah Walker-Dufton and Maryam Ganjineh. Special heartfelt thanks to Rashi and Abhi Sen for their friendship and shared culinary passion.

Acknowledgments

Cover photograph: Restaurant at Souq Madinat Jumeirah, Dubai, Massimo Borchi / Corbis.

This Book

This 4th edition of Lonely Planet's *Pocket Dubai* guidebook was researched and written by Andrea Schulte-Peevers. The previous edition was written by Josephine Quintero and the 2nd edition was written by Olivia Pozzan. This guidebook was produced by the following: **Destination Editor** Helen Elfer **Product Editors** Elin Berglund, Kate Chapman **Regional Senior Cartographer** David Kemp

Book Designer Cam Ashley **Assisting Editors** Kate Evans, Christopher Pitts **Cover Researcher** Naomi Parker **Thanks to** Harry Greenlee, Denis Hallinan, Claire Naylor, Karyn Noble, Katie O'Connell

Index

See also separate subindexes for:

Eating p157

Drinking p158

Entertainment p158

Shopping p158

Sights 000
Map Pages **000**